Management and Organisation in Secondary Schools

A Training Handbook

DEREK TORRINGTON and **JANE WEIGHTMAN**

BLACKWELL EDUCATION

© Derek Torrington, Jane Weightman 1989

First published 1989

Published by Basil Blackwell Ltd
108 Cowley Road
Oxford OX4 1JF
England

British Library Cataloguing in Publication Data
Torrington, Derek, *1931–*
   Management and organisation in secondary schools: a training handbook.
   1. Great Britain. Secondary schools. Management
   I. Title II. Weightman, Jane
   373.12′00941

ISBN 0–631–16761–7

Typeset in 11/13 pt Sabon
by Wearside Tradespools, Fulwell, Sunderland
Printed in Great Britain
by Dotesios Printers Ltd., Trowbridge

Preface

Of the many people who helped our preparation of this book, we are specially grateful to Phillip Adams and Ray Sylvester, who have contributed complete chapters for us, and to Kirsty Johns who had to leave our project before it was completed.

Our other research associates, Roger Clark, John Davnall, Roy Harris and Peter Reid, took a year out of their ordered professional lives to join us in the unfamiliar world of academic study and investigation. Through their shrewd comments they tempered our excesses and shaped our judgement, as well as doing much of the exacting work of interviewing and observation in schools. Throughout our time together they lost neither their appetite for large oriental meals, nor their enthusiastic support for what we were trying to achieve. All of them have contributed draft material which is incorporated in the final version of the book.

Our secretary, Pat Loftus, took on the task of keeping us all under control and in some sort of order, as well as pounding the word processor for hours on end. It is thanks to her that we were able to complete our work on time and within budget.

The investigation which led us to produce these training materials could not have been undertaken without the generous financial support of the Economic and Social Research Council, where we particularly appreciate the advice and interest shown by Martin Kender. James Nash of Basil Blackwell saw the potential for a book in what we were doing and helped us work the material into a viable framework, after which his colleague Marion Casey saw the manuscript through to printed copies.

Our main thanks must, however, go to UMIST for enabling the study to take place, to the local authorities for allowing us to work in their schools, and to the 1065 people who patiently answered our questions and endured our observations in the midst of their hectic working lives. No matter what trials the teaching profession goes through, there can be no more agreeable occupational group of people among whom to work. We appreciate how exceptionally demanding their working lives are, yet they made the process of research unfailingly rewarding for us.

It remains to be seen whether they regard our efforts, in this book and in its companion *The Reality of School Management*, as justifying the time and trouble they took.

Derek Torrington and Jane Weightman
UMIST, Spring 1989

Contents

Section Three: Whole School Reviews –
Managerial and Administrative Initiatives

How to use this book

This introductory chapter has the following sections:

1 Introduction
2 Notes for the trainer
3 Leading group discussion
4 Brainstorming
5 Goal planning

Introduction

This is a companion volume to *The Reality of School Management*, and rooted in the same piece of empirical research on management in schools. Whilst the other book attempts to explain what the researchers observed, here we offer a series of training exercises that draw heavily on the material collected during the research for examples and illustration.

The research was supported by a grant from the Economic and Social Research Council in seeking a review of how management ideas were developing in schools.

Our brief was to study management and organisation in English maintained secondary schools; this produced the shorthand of MOSS to describe our project. Our objective was to develop materials that could be used to assist teachers in the running of their schools. We began, therefore, with the assumption that management and organisation in schools was something undertaken by many people: the study was not directed exclusively at the work of the headteacher or the governors, and did not include the management activities of the local authority.

A key element of the research strategy was the recruitment of research associates to work alongside our own staff, both to extend the range of the fieldwork and to ensure the in-school credibility of our conclusions. After approaching various local authorities we secured a 12 month secondment to our project of six practising teachers: three deputy heads, two heads of department and a main grade teacher.

After intensive preparation during the Summer of 1986, fieldwork began in the Autumn and continued through the following school year, working in 24 maintained secondary schools in Cheshire, Derbyshire, Devon, Dorset, Manchester, Oldham, Salford and Stockport. We spent all day every day for two months in each of the schools, talking to most of the adults working there. Altogether we carried out 1065 in-depth interviews, completed structured observations of the work of 90 individuals, and attended 431 meetings.

The material is targeted generally at school staffs and specifically at those organising training in schools, for whom we use throughout the simple term 'trainer'. Much of the material will also be appropriate for governors and for students. Throughout, the focus is on the internal workings of the school, and especially on the way in which the adults in it work together.

The materials in Section One are designed for individuals to use as self-study guides, to work through ideas on how they tackle the management elements of their jobs and how they could find ways of doing better. Each chapter begins by indicating the sort of person for whom the exercise is appropriate, what should be achieved by completing the exercise, and an estimate of how long it will take. Then there is an exercise with supporting documents.

Section Two contains materials more appropriate for group working. The general approach is similar to that of Section One, but the presentation is designed around the assumption of group discussion as the most common mode of study and analysis. Some of these exercises may be suitable for whole-school INSET.

Section Three is again similar except that it deals with matters of more general interest to those with overall responsibility, such as senior staff.

Notes for the trainer

Each exercise has some notes for the trainer alone, as well as material for distribution. The main skill that the trainer will need is the stimulation and direction of group discussion, although brainstorming and goal planning will also be needed in places. We include notes on both at the end of this introductory chapter; all other notes on methods will be found in the exercises themselves.

The topics and issues covered require thoughtful and sensitive handling, rather than a rigid structure. We are offering a range of materials for trainers to use; not simply exercises for trainers to run. It is the *trainer* who will decide what training is required, how it will be conducted and how its success will be evaluated. Nevertheless, we do make suggestions about how material should be used, and the general approach to be adopted. The main exceptions are chapters 3, 4, 7, 11, 13 and 21, where we believe that the structure we provide is the most appropriate and that the effect of the training could be lost if it were altered without fully calculating both the objectives and the implications of the proposed changes.

We would also suggest that trainers take careful note of the photocopying permission that is included on page ii. All of the chapters include material that will need copying, so please take note of the permission that is granted.

Leading group discussion

Members of a discussion group both compete and co-operate. They will co-operate in the shared task of seeking understanding and developing answers, but they will also compete in wanting to appear shrewd, fluent and perceptive. If there are inequalities of status in the group they will be even more anxious not to appear foolish. Members of the group will look to the Leader for structure at the beginning: a strong indication of how to get started and assistance in developing the social interaction of the group process. As discussion unfolds the Leader will become less obviously necessary to the group, but will still need to control the exchanges to ensure their effectiveness. This sort of control is the hardest part; most teachers are talkative (dare one say voluble?), so they need to be reined in frequently, yet the exercises will only work as learning experiences if it is *their* discussion that takes place. The Leader who squashes people or who imposes a pre-determined 'answer' has failed.

Here is a checklist for trainers leading group discussion:

Before the meeting
a) What do you want the discussion to achieve?
b) How long have you got?
c) What do you know of group members? The following categorisation, modelled on the work of Meredith Belbin, may help:
    The Shaper influences discussion by thoughtful argument and following particular topics.
    The Ideas Person contributes novel suggestions.
    The Radical believes that the group's task cannot begin until something else has been completed – and the 'something else' is always beyond the group's control.
    The Steady Eddy is always cautious and aware of problems.
    The Team Worker keeps the group going by joking when discussion

gets too tense and always finding points on which to agree with other people.

The Monitor likes to review progress and summarise what has been said.

The Shrinking Violet has difficulty in getting into the discussion and is intensely concerned not to sound foolish.

The Completer likes to push things along, get things done and formulate conclusions.

d) Will all group members be able to see and hear each other?

e) Do you have all the necessary materials: hand-outs, flip charts, pencils and paper etc?

During the meeting

a) Does everyone know each other? With a close-knit team, like a senior management group, introductions will obviously not be needed, but there may be a new member of the group or there may be members whose presence puzzles others (or themselves). Sometimes it will be an inter-school group of relative strangers. The group Leader has four basic strategies available:

Assume introductions are not needed.

Introduce individuals 'I think we mostly know each other, but Jan is with us for the first time, having taken up the Head of Humanities post this term. Jan, this is Roger, Head of Science, Sheila, who . . .'

Elicit self-introductions 'Perhaps we could just go round the group, saying who we are and what our role is . . .'

Elicit introductions of others Ask pairs in the group to interview each other for five minutes and then introduce the person they have interviewed to everyone else. The fourth method is particularly useful for strangers, as it initiates discussion and eliminates the self-consciousness felt by many in saying 'I am . . .'

b) How will you introduce the meeting? The Leader needs to set the scene by reminding everyone of why they have assembled and setting out the task to be addressed. At this stage members will welcome clear guidance and structure. The Leader will need to win their consent by signing off with a comment like: 'Is that all right?' 'Is there anything I've missed, do you think?'

c) How will you start off the discussion? The Leader needs to start the discussion by introducing the topic – or the first of several topics – for the group to develop. This may be done by setting out background information, providing factual data, offering an opinion or asking a question. It is wise to move from the general to the particular, by setting up the initial discussion around the broader aspects of the question which can later be brought into much sharper focus.

d) How should you run the discussion? Although the Leader will be less dominant as the discussion gets underway, there is still a need for control, and direction, using the following methods:

Bringing people in The Leader will need to get a balance of views, style and authority in the discussion. Without direction some group members will never speak and others will scarcely stop, but productive discussion will result from a blend of contributions from Shapers, Steady Eddies, Completers and so on. The Leader will not only bring people in in a general way ('What do you think, Frank?') but will also shape the discussion by bringing people in for specific comment ('How does John's idea fit in with what you were saying earlier, Helen?').

Shutting people up Deflating the bombastic is difficult and can make everyone feel awkward if it is not well done, yet the discussion will not work if it is dominated by one or two people. The section on 'Braking' in interviews (page 99) may be helpful, but other techniques for the Leader are to: put one or two closed questions to a person in the middle of a diatribe; give them a job to do ('Could you just jot down for us the main points of that, so that we can come back to it later?'); orientate them towards listening ('Can you see any problems with what Sheila wants to do?').

Focusing discussion There is little need to sustain discussion on matters where everyone agrees. Agreeing with each other is useful for social cohesion, but the Leader will regularly direct discussion back to points of *disagreement*. It helps to bring in someone who has previously been neutral or silent on the matter and who may therefore have a different perspective.

Summarising Periodically the discussion will need summarising and a new direction introduced. Members of the group need to confirm the summary.

Clarification Sometimes a member of the group will make a contribution that others do not understand, so the Leader will seek clarification, ensuring that the responsibility for the confusion is *not* on the person making the statement. 'Could you just go over that again, Fred?' is better than 'I think what Fred is trying to say is . . .'

e) What is the best way to close the discussion? The Leader will pick out from the discussion one or two workable hypotheses or points of general consensus and put them to the meeting for acceptance. Group members will look to the Leader for that type of closure so that they have confirmation that their time has been well spent: only the Leader can really see the wood for the trees. The best discussions finish on time!

Brainstorming

Brainstorming is a specialised technique for developing a range of new ideas for examination. At several points in the book it is suggested as an appropriate training aid. You need a flip chart, blackboard or overhead projector and someone who can write quickly and legibly.

Before the meeting
a) Decide the purpose of the session. Is it:
  - to find uses for a new idea?
  - to generate a range of new ideas?
  - to find a better way of doing something? or
  - to find a solution to a problem?
b) Make notes of your own preliminary ideas.

Running the meeting – Generation
a) Appoint a note-taker.
b) Introduce the purpose of the meeting and ask group members to call out any idea that comes into their heads.
c) Write ideas on flip chart so that all members can see them.
d) Encourage members to develop the ideas of others ('hitch-hiking') as well as 'sparking' in different directions.
e) Ban judgement. All ideas are valid, however bizarre, even if they seem to be repeating what has already been said. Even such subtle judgements as laughter, gasps of disbelief and nods of approval can inhibit or direct thinking. All should be banned at this stage.
f) Generate momentum, so that the group keeps going.
g) Reach a target number of ideas – say 65 – in 15 to 30 minutes.

Running the meeting – Classification
a) Collectively classify the ideas into five or six groups, possibly adding others suggested by the classification.
b) Ask the group to rank the ideas in each classification against questions such as:
  - how new?
  - how relevant?
  - how feasible?

Goal planning

Goal planning is a simple technique for moving ideas into action. It is recommended at several points in the book. This is the drill:

a) Decide what particular goal you want to achieve, or what change you want to make.

b) Write down the criteria you will use to decide whether you have been successful.
c) Make a list (see example below) of strengths and needs, needs being what has to be met to achieve your goal and strengths being what will help you in meeting the goal. Write these as concretely as possible so that you can tell when you have met a need – which then becomes a strength.

Goal: Run a training session for HoDs on appraisal interviewing using Chapter 10 'Appraisal'.

STRENGTHS	NEEDS
1. 3 hrs set aside on INSET day in September. 2. LEA and staff talking about appraisal.	1. Use of library that day. 2. Agreement of other senior staff. 3. Co-operation of all HoDs. 4. Train myself on the materials. 5. Photocopy materials.

d) Take one of your needs that is particularly difficult to achieve. Break it down into smaller objectives on the form below.

Need 3 Co-operation of all HoDs.

OBJECTIVE	METHOD OF TACKLING	TARGET DATE	DATE DONE
Inform them about LEA/School policy	Get time at next HoD meeting to discuss appraisal and implications	Week on Wed.	
Need for training at HoD level	Talk to each HoD individually	End of month.	
Get HT and DHTs to emphasise delegation to HoD of appraisal	See each of them informally and ask them to reinforce my message.	Tomorrow.	

Section One

SELF-DEVELOPMENT MATERIALS

The five sets of material in this section are designed mainly for individual self-development, although all of them could be used in groups, with careful adaptation by the trainer. The overall purpose of the materials is for individuals to reflect on how they set about their management duties and begin to see ways of improvement. The exercises provided are:

1 Credibility: how those with privilege win respect
   Notes for personal study and reflection
2 sTAMp: getting the right balance between the various components of the management job
   Structured analysis of one's current work pattern
3 Agendas and networks: establishing what needs doing and creating contacts to make it happen
   Methods of management improvement
4 Valuing: consideration, delegation and participation
   Notes for personal study and reflection
5 Team management: the Head of Department function
   Methods of management improvement

1 Credibility: how those with privilege win respect

This short chapter addresses a matter of concern to all those seen by their colleagues as 'privileged'. It is intended to help you clarify some aspects of your working relationships with colleagues and enable you to win a constructive response from them. Winning that type of response is the basis of being an effective manager in dealing with other people.

On completion you should be able to:

a) understand the concepts of *credibility* and *privilege* as they affect the way in which managers do their jobs;
b) identify those privileges you enjoy which affect your credibility;
c) enhance your personal credibility to improve your management effectiveness.

You will need:

Credibility Document I — *An example of gaining credibility*

Introduction

There is a potential credibility problem for those with privilege in schools, yet all adults in school need credibility to be effective. The main features of 'privilege' for adults in school are some or all of: larger salaries, less contact time, smaller classes, 'easier' classes, less marking, non-teaching assistance, having one's own room, having one's own telephone (particularly with an outside line). The nature of classroom credibility is familiar to all teachers. Management credibility in schools is similar in concept, but different in method.

The main features of the *management credibility* concept are:

1 A person with credibility among colleagues is trustworthy, convincing, respected, and will be believed.
2 Credibility is related to authority by increasing the degree of personal influence on events and making one's power legitimate.
3 Credibility is not a right that comes with the job, nor an intrinsic

quality of the individual. It has to be earned and sustained by each person in each new position.

4 A person with high credibility has influence among the adults in the school, is listened to and can get done willingly things that may not otherwise be done at all.

5 A person with low credibility has to rely only on formal mechanisms and procedures to get things done and lowers the morale of those working with them.

The following are particularly prone to credibility problems: individuals with reduced timetables (eg those responsible for cross-school new initiatives); Special Needs support staff, English as a second language and Section 11 staff; Senior teachers and Deputy Heads. (Heads and Heads of Department are less likely to have such problems.)

Your personal credibility checklist

Document I and the following questions will help you examine your own credibility.

1 Is your position in the school one which is likely to present problems of personal credibility in the eyes of your colleagues? Remember, credibility is primarily a function of the *role* rather than the person.

2 Is there any evidence in recent weeks of you lacking credibility? Forget your paranoia or your self-doubts and think about tangible *evidence*? If so, write down a list of the incidents that have occurred.

3 What aspects of your role is the evidence connected to? (eg small classes, light timetable or something else)

4 What are the effects of your lack of credibility: on your contribution to the school? on your colleagues? on yourself?

5 How can your credibility in your present position be enhanced? The example of Derek in Credibility Document I may offer some ideas. Other possibilities include:
- making your role and duties better known to people;
- taking care not to flaunt your privileges;
- reviewing your contribution to the school to be sure that it matches your privileges.
- sharing privileges, whilst taking care not to be condescending. ('Can you help me with the timetable . . .?' is very different from 'Providing you don't make a mess, you can use my kettle when I don't need it.')

Now decide on two or three things to do in the next fortnight, and move on to the next chapter in this book.

Credibility document I
An example of gaining credibility

William Barnes was a well-established school with very low staff turnover. Most of the staff had spent all their teaching career (often more than 20 years) in the school. The Deputy Head/Pastoral was a pillar of this establishment who dealt with discipline problems amongst the children loudly and clearly. Staff relied on him to back them up and felt secure that discipline would be firm. He retired at the end of the summer term and Derek arrived as his replacement the following September.

Derek was 33, younger than most of the staff, and he was appointed from outside the school and its immediate neighbours. He was tall, dark and handsome. By the time the researchers arrived in November, Derek had established a lot of respect. Teachers kept saying, 'You must go and see Derek, he's marvellous'. In terms of credibility with the staff, Derek had 'a tough act to follow'. How had he done it?

The basis of his acceptance was lots of small, but important things:

- He was *reliable* – if he said he would do something he did it.
- He was *consistent*, treating people issues fairly and predictably.
- He *set up order* where it had previously been lacking, such as systems for reports and examination entries.
- He was *visible*, regularly walking about in the building, playground, dining room.
- He *took up individual problems* but only after checking that the appropriate system, procedure or person had been tried first.

© Derek Torrington, Jane Weightman, Basil Blackwell Ltd, 1989.

2 sTAMp: getting the right balance between the various components of the management job

Those doing management jobs spend their time on work of different types. They often spend a disproportionate amount of time on work that is relatively trivial or even unnecessary. The self-development exercise set out here is a way of both analysing how you spend your time and making changes in emphasis that will give you a better degree of control over what you do.

On completion you should be able to:

a) analyse the balance of your work;
b) understand the value of doing technical work;
c) understand the problem of doing too much administrative work;
d) plan changes in the balance of your work, where appropriate.

You will need:

sTAMp Document I – *Time spent by three Deputy Heads*
sTAMp Document II – *Record of time spent*
sTAMp Document III – *Percentage of time spent by 70 senior staff*

Introduction

One way of analysing the work of individual managers is to distinguish between their technical, administrative and managerial work:

Technical work is that work that managers do because of their profession, experience or qualification. In schools this means teaching, preparing and marking the children's work, anything involving the children directly and discussing curriculum with colleagues.

Administrative work is concerned with organisational maintenance. It is carrying out official, often regular, duties authorised by others; it is usually clerical work. In schools this includes filling in returns, making lists, putting out chairs in the hall, trying to get through on the telephone, drawing graphs, using the photocopier and sorting out papers.

Managerial work is that work a manager does which entails setting precedents. It often involves influencing others to assent to some non-obvious decision or behaviour. It is getting something done that would not otherwise have been done. In schools this involves such things as discussing with teachers how the timetable can be better next year, regrouping the children in the third year, walking round the school to pick up on what is happening, deciding the agenda for a meeting.

Managers also spend time on *social* activities which are the everyday social interchanges of organisational life. It is an essential part of anyone's work to create and sustain a sufficient network of social contacts to get the job done. Some time has to be spent on purely *personal* matters, such as telephone calls with a spouse or fixing an appointment for the car to be serviced. Someone doing administration will also do managerial work. All managers' jobs contain all of these elements, no manager would have a zero for any category.

To clarify the distinction between these categories look at Document I: *Time spent by three Deputy Heads*.

Document I: Time spent by three Deputy Heads

1 The various activities of the three people observed are categorised as s, T, A, M, p. Would you categorise any of them differently? Much depends on the individual judgement of the person doing the categorisation, but you will probably not want to change more than 1 in 10.
2 Which of the three do you regard as most effective in the role of Deputy Head, on the basis of the limited evidence provided here?
3 For each of the three, list the activities which you feel should have been dealt with by someone else, where the Deputy could personally have arranged for the other person to do it.
4 If the three Deputies had delegated to others the activities you have listed, do you think they would have made better use of the time saved?

Document II: Recording time spent

Analyse how you spend your time, using Document II: *Recording time spent*.

1 Record how you spend your time at work for at least one day. Try to do it during the day in question and not later, as small details are easily forgotten.

2 Every time you change an activity, start a new line. A change of activity is either moving to a new topic or a new person. Meetings count as one activity, so does teaching (unless interrupted from outside).

3 Some activities have to be scored hybrid, eg T/M, as they are both technical and managerial. Try to keep these to a minimum. Count 'walkabout' as Managerial.

Making sense of the data

Add up the total number of activities and the time spent on each.

Document III shows the time distribution of senior staff we observed. How does your time analysis compare with these findings? Your information can now be analysed in various ways:

1 Does your day fit that described by Mintzberg (1973) as typical, with constant interruptions and only brief periods devoted to any one topic?

2 What surprises you about the time distribution?

3 How much of your day was spent responding to others and how much was spent initiating contacts with others?

4 How much was spent face-to-face and how much alone?

5 What proportion of your day was spent on each of technical, administrative and managerial work?

6 What aspects of your answers to questions 1 to 5 do you find unsatisfactory?

7 How do you get greater control over how your time is spent, so that your contribution to the running of the school is enhanced and your working day provides you with more satisfaction?

Conclusion

All managers need periodically to examine the balance of their work. It is important that those with senior posts maintain their *technical* work for several reasons:

1 It is a source of personal satisfaction in (still) being able to do well the job for which they are professionally qualified.

2 It is the only way of really keeping in touch with the school's work.

3 It is the basis of being an authority through expertise.

4 It is important for the school – ensuring that experienced, able teachers continue to work with the pupils.

5 It is important for other members of staff that those in senior posts

maintain their technical work, as they can seek advice from those seen to have current experience of what the problems are.

The *administrative* work that senior staff do can create serious problems for both them and the school, if it becomes excessive.

1 When senior staff are seen doing a lot of clerical work their authority and credibility with other members of staff is undermined – particularly as non-teaching staff, who have been trained in this type of work, can usually do it more effectively.
2 Administrative work offers a manager the spurious attraction of actually being able to complete something. Getting to the bottom of a pile or completing a list can be comforting in an otherwise hectic day in which everything else seems to have gone wrong. Some administrative work is therefore necessary, but too much introduces inadequate criteria of success.
3 Staff promoted to management posts look round for the new tasks that come with the job. Often the most obvious are the administrative tasks listed in the job description. This can lead to managers creating more administrative work in the mistaken belief that this is what management is about. They may miss the intangible essence through focusing on the tangible trivia.
4 Administrative work frequently requires an input (a list, a set of documents, or similar data) from someone else. There is always the risk that this is making unnecessary work for other people.

The *managerial* work of senior staff is always the more uncertain, difficult, challenging and important.

1 Because it is about making things happen that would not otherwise happen, all sorts of different skills are involved.
2 Where policy making, decision taking, communications, personnel issues and procedures are all concentrated in the hands of the Headteacher it can be very difficult indeed for other senior staff to see what their managerial work might be.
3 Managerial work, as described in these notes, is mainly created by the job holder. Even though responsibilities may be assigned to the job holder by others, no-one else can 'make it happen'.

References

Mintzberg, H, *The Nature of Managerial Work*, Harper and Row, London, 1973.
Stewart, R, *Choices for Managers*, McGraw-Hill, Maidenhead, 1982.
Torrington, D. and Weightman, J, 'Middle Management Work', *Journal of General Management*, 1988.

sTAMp Document I: Time spent by three Deputy Heads

A Deputy Head I

	% of Time				
	s	T	A	M	p
Day	2	3	19	76	0
Hour	2	2	36	57	0

Time	Activity	Who with	Init. self/ other	sTAMp
8.40	Conversation with Head re problem pupil	Head	Other	M
8.50	Informing members of staff re problem pupil	Self so far	Self	M
8.54	Spoke to pupil about a problem	Pupil	Other	T/M
8.55	Spoke to caretaker about workmen	Caretaker	Other	A
8.58	Gave pupil a piece of paper	Pupil	Other	A
8.59	Went off to find and inform some members of staff	Teachers	Self	A
9.00	Came back to room to answer telephone	Parent/Secretary	Other	M
9.01	Joan brought in a cup of coffee for him	Joan	Other	S
9.02	Alice came in with slip for him re pupil	Alice	Other	A
9.04	Pat came in with a query	Pat	Other	A
9.04	Tried to get Ray on internal tannoy	Self – no answer	Self	A
9.06	Discussed 3rd Year Option brochure	Jean	Other	M
9.10	Answered telephone, Ray	Ray	Other	M
9.10	Discussed brochure with Head and Jean	Head, Jean	Other	M
9.11	Discussed TRIST cover problems with Jean	Jean	Other	M
9.12	Phoned the office re register	Secretary	Self	A
9.13	Left office to go to office	Secretary	Self	A
9.15	Started work on options brochure	Self	Self	M
9.19	Pupil question at door	Pupil	Other	T
9.20	Answered phone – secretary announcing arrival of parent	Secretary	Other	A
9.24	Parent arrived for confidential interview re child. Researcher left	Parent	Other	

B Deputy Head II

	s	T	A	M	p
		% of Time			
Day	0.5	23	47	29	0
Hour	1.0	0	75	24	0

Time	Activity	Who with	Init. self/ other	sTAMp
8.20	Fed available data for cover into computer in secretary's office	Self	Self	A
8.30	Returned to own room to sort out messages for announcements	Self	Self	A/M
8.32	Went out to speak to Ian re appointment with a parent	Ian	Self	A
8.34	Returned to room to write out timetable for supply teachers	Self	Self	A
8.35	Peter (DH1) popped head round to remark upon some aspect of the previous night's meeting	Peter	Other	M/S
8.36	Continued, then went on to prepare notices for announcements	Self	Self	A/M
8.37	Back to secretary's office to print out first 'go' of cover by computer	Self	Self	A/M
8.38	Was asked to go to the phone – refused	Sec, 4 YTS	Other	A
8.38+	School Secretary 1 informed her of another staff absence message	Secretary 1	Other	A
8.39	School Secretary 4 (YTS) came in with another staff absence message	Secretary 4 YTS	Other	A
8.40	Went back to her office to consult her notes	Self	Self	A
8.41	Returned to re-type the information into the computer for second go	Self	Self	A
8.44	Returned to her office to finalise messages	Self	Self	A/M
8.45	Gave messages to YHds on phone (internal)		Self	A
8.46	Secretary 1 brought in list of staff not yet signed in	Secretary	Other	A
8.46	John came in with more information on staff arrivals	John	Other	A

Time	Activity	Who with	Init. self/other	sTAMp
8.46+	All this time Mary was relaying messages to all year staff	Self, all Year Heads through internal phones	Self	A/M
8.49	Back to secretary's room to print out cover slips	Self	Self	A
8.51	Back to own office to cut up cover slips	Self	Self	A
8.53	Back to secretary's office to alter, update cover totals in programme	Self	Self	A
8.55	Finished in office (secs). Wrote up cover list in full for Peter and Joan's information	Self	Self	A
8.58	Took a printed copy of the cover to pin on the board in the staffroom	Self	Self	A
8.59	Back to office to phone back Education Offices – the call refused earlier	Official in LEA office	Self?	A
9.02	Pupil called to discuss a Christmas activity. Pupil called to pick up a cover slip	Pupil	Other	A
9.03	Paul came in, query re orals (French)	Paul	Other	A
9.04	Supply teacher called to pick up timetable	Supply	Other	A
9.05	Sec 1 came in to approve draft letter	Secretary 1	Other	A/M
9.10	Alan came in to query whether getting too many cover periods	Alan	Other	M
9.12	Ian came in to discuss pastoral matters	Ian	Other	M
9.14	Researcher left to allow her to interview a parent			

C Deputy Head III (in same school as B)

	s	T	A	M	p
		% of Time			
Day	7	0	42	49	0
Hour	0	0	30	70	0

Time	Activity	Who with	Init. self/ other	sTAMp
9.00	Resumed preparation for Presentation Evening	Alone	Self	A/M
9.07	Returned cups to office	Alone	Self	A
9.08	Spoke to Susie	Susie	Self	A
9.09	Ran to Sl Needs Dept. Spoke to Philip	Philip	Self	A

9.10	Spoke to Jane re theft	Jane	Self	M
9.14	Walked through rain back to room	Alone	Self	A
9.15	Dealing with admin, for Physics scale 3 post	Self	Self	A
9.18	Checked return slips for Presentation Evening	Self	Self	A
9.19	Took application details to clerk for posting off	Joan	Self	A
9.20	Checked off a return slip for Presentation Evening	Self	Self	A
9.21	Pupil arrived with a Presentation Evening return slip	Pupil	Other	A
9.21	Checked off the pupil's return slip	Self	Self	A
9.22	Off to see how many tables in Arthur's room	Self	Self	A
9.25	Spoke to Arthur re tables for mock exams	Arthur	Self	A
9.25	Spoke to Mrs S re Jane investigation of theft	Mrs S	Self	M
9.27	Interviewed pupil in his office	Pupil	Self	M
9.31	Dismissed pupil, spoke to the interpreter, dismissed	Asian pupil interpreting	Self	M
9.35	Jane arrived with another pupil and another interpreter re theft	Jane	Other	M
9.36	Began to interview second pupil re theft	Pupil	Self	M
9.41	Dismissed the pupil	Pupil	Self	M
9.41	Spoke to Jane in her room re theft	Jane	Self	M
9.47	Went to speak to Head, who had popped head in door	Head	Other	M
9.48	Went to clerk to ask her to type s.t.	Joan	Self	A
9.50	Jane arrived with another pupil to interview	Jane	Other	M
9.51	Began to interview pupil through interpreter re theft	Asian pupil	Self	M
9.58	Dismissed this pupil, began to interview another pupil	Another Asian pupil	Self	M
10.05	Dismissed this pupil	Pupil	Self	M

sTAMp Document II: Record of time spent

Time	Activity	With	Initiated	sTAMp work	Notes

sTAMp Document III: Percentage of time spent by 70 senior staff on different activities

	% of time				
	s	T	A	M	p

6 Headteachers and Acting Headteachers

	s	T	A	M	p
Mean	2.8	23	11	60.7	1.3
Range	0–6	3–64	4–18	27–82	0–4

33 Deputy Headteachers and Acting Deputy Headteachers

	s	T	A	M	p
Mean	5	21.2	31.27	39.3	2.6
Range	1–14	0–50	12–77	4–76	0–24

7 Senior Teachers

	s	T	A	M	p
Mean	5.4	33.3	27	30.9	2.4
Range	0–10	11–54	9–48	10–50	0–14

12 Heads of House/Year/parts of school

	s	T	A	M	p
Mean	4.4	37.6	29.2	22.9	3.4
Range	0–23	9–62	2–58	5–65	0–12

10 Heads of Department/Faculty/Curriculum Area

	s	T	A	M	p
Mean	6.4	33.8	24	28.1	4.2
Range	3–14	0–67	7–53	15–56	0–16

2 Joint Heads of Subject and Pastoral Team

	s	T	A	M	p
Mean	9	48	18	24	1.5
Range	2–16	44–52	15–21	9–38	0–3

3 Agendas and networks: establishing what needs doing and creating contacts to make it happen

Having got a fix on the type of work you do, and begun the process of bringing it under better control, you can now take a further step in organising your time and improving your effectiveness. This exercise is suitable for all those with responsibility in schools, but we have found it especially useful for Heads of Department, Pastoral Heads and Deputy Heads.

The materials in the last chapter required you to record and analyse your activities in order to classify them: this exercise requires you simply to sit down and work things out on paper. You may be tempted to do this exercise before Chapter two, but we strongly advise that you move on to these materials only *after* completing the exercise in Chapter two.

On completion you should be able to:

a) organise your time better;
b) understand the importance of informal contacts;
c) get things done more effectively.

You will need:

Agenda/network Document I – *Your agenda*
Agenda/network Document II – *Your network of contacts*

Introduction

Kotter (1982) examined the role of general managers and defined their core behaviour as first setting agendas for action and then establishing and maintaining networks to implement these agendas.

Agendas are lists of things to be done, written or not, thought out or not, short-term and long-term. They come about by generating possibilities, questioning plans and proposals, gathering information and calculating ways and means of implementing policies, plans, strategies and agreements. A useful analogy is the checklist of jobs to be done before going on holiday: stop the papers, stop the milk, service the car, check the rubber dinghy, find the pump, book the dog into kennels, and so forth. Managers work through a similar set of agendas every day, with new items constantly being added and some being 'crossed off'. These are all the things to do and get done, but which never all get done.

Networks are sets of contacts built up with those working inside and outside the organisation: current and previous colleagues, the bosses' boss and the subordinates' subordinates and many other people within the company and in other companies, customers, suppliers, members of professional bodies and so forth. They are co-operative relationships with people who can help to get things done. The networks Kotter's managers developed included hundreds or thousands of people and every relationship was different. The network is for sharing ideas, information and resources.

This simple analytical device can be used to examine the work of those with management responsibility in schools, as it emphasises the reality of how things get done rather than the popular misconception of managers as calmly sitting in offices creating formal plans, control systems and structures, with action following effortlessly after decision.

Your agenda

1 Make a list as instructed in Document I, on *'Your agenda'*. (This takes about 20 to 30 minutes.)
2 Analyse the items on your agenda. This can be done in various ways:
   - Classify the items on the agenda into:
     Must do
     Should do
     Would like to do
   Use your classification for time management by listing when during the week, the 'must do' will get done.
   - Classify the items on the agenda into:
     Demands from others I must do
     Demands from others that can be dealt with elsewhere
     Choices of mine I must do
     Choices of mine that others could do
   Review the differences between demands and choices; things I must do and things that can be dealt with elsewhere. Rosemary Stewart discusses demands and choices for managers in her book *Choices for managers* (McGraw Hill, 1982).
3 Review your lists in the light of the sTAMp analysis of the previous chapter:
   Are you allowing the urgent to take precedence over the important?

Do your priorities reflect a good TAM balance?
Are you and others doing the right mix of items on the agenda according to your different skills, interests and positions?
4 Repeat the classification in a week's time; decide what you have learned and identify the ways in which your agendas can improve. Thereafter repeat the exercise regularly, ideally once a month.

Networks

1 Fill in Document II with all the individuals or groups who affect how effective you are in your job, with whom you have a formal or an informal relationship. Give both names and positions. The drawing, which may look something like the one on Document II, will describe your network.
2 Work through the tasks on the second page of the document.

References

Kotter, J, *The General Managers*, The Free Press, 1982.
Stewart, R, *Choices for Managers*, McGraw Hill, 1982.

Agenda/network Document I: Your agenda

1 List all the things you *should* do at work in the next week. Write them down as they occur to you. Include:
Major long-term aims
Short-term projects
Regular items
Trivia that needs to be done

2 Now add to this list all those things – big and small – that you *would like* to do at work next week.

3 Is there anything else that you *could* do at work because you want to or someone else wants you to? Add these.

4 How does this fit in with the expressed plans for your Department, the school, the LEA?

5 How much of this agenda is there because you want it? How much because you think it will help someone else out?

Agenda/network Document II: Your network of contacts

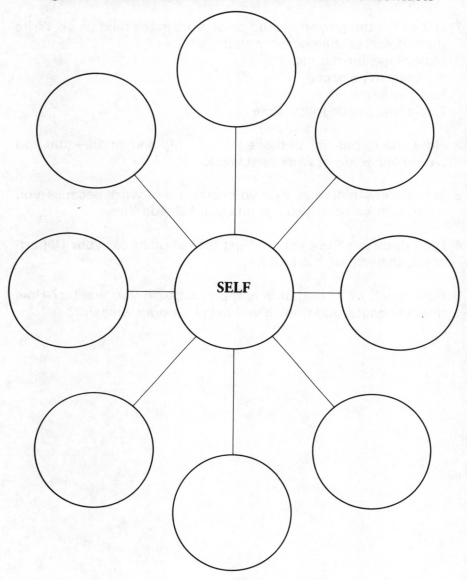

On the chart:

1 Rank order the contacts in your network, formal and informal, in their importance to you in getting your job done effectively.
2 Rate each contact on a scale between −3 and +3, according to how helpful the person is to you.
3 What can be done to improve relationships with those you have rated between −1 and −3?
4 Who else do you need to add to your network in order to implement your agendas more effectively?
5 How are you going to make these additions? Write yourself an agenda for developing your personal network over the next four weeks.

Rank	Contact	−3	−2	−1	0	1	2	3	Improved by
1									
2									
3									
4									
5									
6									
7									
8									
9									

4 Valuing: consideration, delegation and participation

This chapter is presented among other self-development materials as we feel that successful valuing can only be achieved by individual initiative and response to colleagues, which is an opportunity and responsibility of every adult in the school. The materials can also be used in group situations if the trainer feels this more appropriate. It is important, however, that the outcome should be individuals deciding how they personally value their colleagues, rather than assuming it is to be done by someone else.

On completion you should be able to:

a) identify strategies for improving the staffroom;
b) have a larger number of ways of valuing other staff.

You will need:

Valuing Document I – *A Staffroom*
Valuing Document II – *Gary*

Introduction

Most teachers feel under-valued by their fellow citizens. Partly they are sharing in the situation of other employed people, as there has been a general levelling out of status differentials, if not of pay differentials. But the particular situation of teachers' low self-esteem has been aggravated by the acrimony of long-running industrial action and widespread dissatisfaction with government policies on education. This feeling of low appreciation from outside makes it much more important for teachers to be valued by their colleagues inside the school.

At the same time as teachers feel less appreciated by the world outside, the innovations to which schools are being required to respond, generated largely by that same world outside, have multiplied in recent years. Bolam (1986) listed as many as 40 'current changes (innovations, policy initiatives and developments) which have to be managed' – and that was before the national curriculum, local financial management, the new contract and so on. Seldom will all these apply simultaneously to a school, but never before have secondary schools had to cope with so many changes, many of them major. The fact that most of these changes are landing on schools from outside means that staff feel little or no 'ownership' of them. This not only reduces the likelihood of changes being implemented effectively, it also demoralises by creating a sense of being at the mercy of others. Many of the changes require staff to adjust their working practices, and nearly all of them are generating increased workloads. Most schools are suffering from innovation overload, just at a time when staff morale is – generally speaking – lower than it has been for years.

Staff are responding to this situation in different ways; some by withholding commitment, some by withdrawing from out-of-school activities, some by increased militancy, some by reduced militancy, some simply bow their heads and resolve to work harder – again – like Boxer the horse in *Animal Farm*. We encountered many staff who seem to have stoically decided to concentrate on doing their best to tackle the major, inescapable tasks that face them.

Four types of valuing need to be examined in discussing adult relationships within schools: consideration, feedback, delegation and consultation.

Consideration

Two teachers said to us:

> *The children are not motivated to work and teachers get disillusioned. There's no help from senior staff. If we got more support such as 'homework in lower school must be done' it would be better.*

> *No-one supports me here. No-one talks to you in the staffroom. It is not friendly with folk across departments. I'd rather go and read a book.*

Teachers tend to feel a lack of consideration from their colleagues when the school culture is one of keeping to oneself rather than talking to colleagues, even at the level of simple things such as eye contact in the corridors, 'good mornings', smiling and the other everyday courtesies of the working day. To the researcher this is one of the most marked variations in culture between schools.

It may be that these acts of consideration are not common because staff feel it inappropriate to the idea of the independent, professional teacher. But our evidence suggests that most teachers would welcome more of these small gestures and that they are important in the school setting. To the outsider it may seem a minor issue, but to the teachers themselves it is clearly very significant. The American researcher

Herzberg (1968) made the shrewd observation that those aspects of the working situation which *dissatisfy* us are what he called 'hygiene factors' in that they infect the whole working performance. When, however, they are removed, other features of work may motivate us. Lack of consideration in schools seems to be the biggest of all 'dissatisfiers'.

Read Document I – *A Staffroom* and answer the following questions:

1 What do you do to make people feel valued?
2 What about the staffroom?
3 What about the coffee facilities?
4 What would you do about the staffroom in Document I?
5 Imagine you have a budget of £400. How would you spend it, given the following prices?

Chairs £30 each	Curtains £50
Carpet £200	Kettle £20
Fridge £100	Bookcase £50
Coffee machine £150	Employing someone £2 per hour

6 What else would you do?

Feedback

The second type of valuing is concerned with feedback, evaluation and appraisal. The teacher, in company with many other professionals, lacks tangible indicators of success because the output of 'a good teacher' defies measurement, just as 'a good school' defies definition. A company director can refer to the annual profit figures, the entertainer can look at the size of the audience and the writer can look at the level of sales, but the teacher does not have such simple, if misleading, yardsticks of personal achievement. All too often the enormous contribution and exhausting effort seems to lack any perceptible output. Like anyone else the teacher wants an answer to the question, 'How am I doing?' There are many instances when the children provide much-cherished valuing through their spontaneous warmth or sudden spurts of progress, but these have to be balanced against instances of rudeness, boredom and sullenness. Few human groups can be quite so unexpectedly brutal as a group of children dealing with an adult.

Teachers need feedback from other teachers. But they have ambivalent attitudes towards it. They see that it can provide reassurance and encouragement, or it may destroy self-confidence.

Many staff we interviewed said that they did not see enough of the boss, and no-one seemed interested in what they were doing. If appraisal was positive and supportive, in a climate of trust, they would welcome the chance to let the world know what they were doing. Some find teaching a lonely job and need reassurance that they are working appropriately despite their own worries and sense of insecurity,

> The English Department at William Barnes School was well established, many of its members having been in post for 20 years. The Head of Department was described as a gentleman. He systematically saw each member of this large department for a period each half term to talk about their classes and what they wanted to develop in the future within the department.

1 Do you think the system at William Barnes School is a good one?
2 In what ways, apart from formal appraisal, would you give feedback to people in your school?

Delegation

> *The Head of Department is very appreciative of what I do. So is the Head. He sends me little notes occasionally. Recognition of this sort is important because teaching is such a lonely job, but the most important sort of recognition is being given real responsibility.*

Members of staff are valued when responsibility is delegated to them, but this involves delegating *real responsibility* down the hierarchy, not just giving people jobs to do. Teachers must be trusted to make decisions about whether, what and how to do things, not just given the work of filling in lists or teaching new courses. Also responsibility cannot be delegated and then taken away without devaluing the person and destroying their confidence and future effectiveness.
  Read Document II:

1 What would you delegate to Gary?
2 How would you go about this?

Consultation and participation

In view of the innovation overload referred to already, it will be difficult to create the conditions in which teachers can respond to changes with enthusiasm. However, if they wish to respond with commitment rather than mere stoical compliance, there is scope within schools for a participative style of implementation that creates a sense of ownership of the 'how' of innovation even if there is no sense of ownership of the 'what'. Where the Head and close colleagues react to innovation overload without offering participation, it is likely that change will be implemented formally. This will involve precise specification of what everyone else should do from the in-school innovator, who will have acquired some ownership of the change at the same time as denying ownership to colleagues. Implementation may then be patchy and laborious. Consultation makes the early stages of innovation slower, but the later stages are quicker and more effective.

The nature of consultation and participation is affected by *structures* (see material on organisation charts and timetabling); by *processes* (see material on meetings and communication) and by the *consultative performance* of people in key positions (see material on credibility and sTAMp).

1 List five or six innovations there have been in your school during the last few weeks.
2 Against each indicate whether the degree of consultation was sufficient or insufficient, effective or ineffective.
3 Could any of the innovations have been implemented better if there had been more or less consultation? How?
4 List two or three innovations coming to the school shortly.
5 What type of consultation, if any, is appropriate for each?

Conclusion

Most management initiatives in school depend on the lead of those in key positions. Valuing is different as at least some of its elements can come from any source, especially consideration and feedback. Furthermore consideration by, and feedback from, one person tends to elicit consideration and feedback responses from others. Responsibility for consideration and feedback does not have to be delegated from others; we all share it. Here are some examples:

> The Head of Department who asked another departmental head for suggestions on computer usage – 'because you seem to do it better than we do' – not only got some useful suggestions, but also a reciprocal request for a combined team teaching initiative – 'because we had not realised how far on you were'.
>
> The Department that had an Open Day for colleagues to come and see some of their work and make suggestions for improvement.
>
> The Probationary Teacher who said to a teacher after helping with a lesson, 'I'm sure I'll never be able to do that,' received much more helpful and constructive suggestions after making the comment than before.

Valuing Document I: A staffroom

Not only is the present staffroom a sad little place – it is in the wrong place! It is situated in the bottom left hand corner of the school, up some stairs above the admin block; about as far away as you can get from the main teaching areas.

It occupies a space about 13′×12′ in which there is just room for six shabby armchairs, a 9′ upholstered bench, a narrow worktop, some lockers, the staff pigeonholes and, in the centre, two coffee tables piled high with back copies of the TES, school journey brochures and assorted flotsam and jetsam. Noticeboards which cover two walls carry general information and notices from the NUT and NAS/UWT. These are kept reasonably tidy. On the worktop is the staff telephone and a series of racks designed to carry the school report folders. In the corner is a small sink containing some mugs which do not seem to have been washed for about five years (which happens to be the last time the place was used for drinking tea or coffee).

Five years ago the staffroom was three times as big since it incorporated the room next door. At that time the space occupied by the present room was the Quiet/Marking room, off the main staffroom and separated by a movable screen. Five years ago the Consultative Committee (the main staff forum) voted the bulk of the staffroom out of existence to become a typing or keyboard skills room. At that time nobody could find any substantive reasons for keeping it because few teachers, apart from the smokers, actually used it. The school is socially compartmentalised, not because the staffroom is small and smoky, but because most departments have a convenient cubbyhole which they can call their own. Most staff only come to the staffroom to collect their mail and peruse the noticeboards. This is partly because it is too far to travel to the staffroom for the single break of the day. Tales are told of the nice dinner lady who 'got the hump' and withdrew her kettle which she used to make tea and coffee for the staff. Following this walk out the staff tried, for a time, to organise their own tea and coffee facilities. Apparently this effort failed because nobody was prepared to collect the money for the materials.

Valuing Document II: Gary

Gary was in his late twenties, teaching Maths and Computing. His enthusiasm for computing had led him to develop all sorts of systems for whole-school use; for example, lists of children, timetabling, examination options. He had a knack of seeing where computing could relieve teachers of day-to-day administrative tasks. A computing system was introduced into the administration office by the Head, in consultation with the LEA, and Gary was not involved at all. He could not understand why his experience and expertise were not consulted. He started putting satiric writing on the staff noticeboard and was becoming embittered. If someone had either used his skills to aid the introduction of computing in administration or explained why he was not being included, perhaps his energies could still be organisationally functional whereas they were in danger of becoming dysfunctional.

- *What would you do, now, to keep Gary involved in the school?*

5 Team management: the Head of Department function
Phillip Adams

This material, like that in chapter 4, could be used for group work as well as for individual study, but is directed specifically at Heads of Department or those aspiring to that role. It aims to improve understanding of the management responsibilities and management methods appropriate to this particular type of role in the school.

On completion you should be able to:

a) have a clearer idea of the role of Head of Department, and awareness of suitable management methods;
b) appreciate colleagues' conception of the post of Head of Department, and their expectations of the post-holder.

You will need:

Team management Document I: *Credibility*
Team management Document II: *Quality control*
Team management Document III: *Effective departments*

Introduction

Research indicates that many secondary schools are well run, with many good management practices. At the same time many schools clearly have problems, among which these stand out:

1 Observation and interviews reveal that the greatest constraint on staff is shortage of time. The rational response to time pressure is to prioritise tasks, but often staff priorities differ from management priorities, leading to conflict and stress.
2 Schools are suffering from 'innovation overload'. Never have schools been expected to absorb so much change, imposed by the government from outside. At the same time they are being expected to generate their own internal schemes (for instance CPVE, Records of Achievement).
3 The fact that most of the changes emanate from outside the school, combined with the pace of the required changes, can lead to

insufficient staff 'ownership' of what is happening, with a feeling of insufficient consultation, even a sense of alienation, leading to cynicism.

4 Partly as a result of the long period of union action, the gulf between the Head plus Deputies and the rest of the staff has often widened. This intensifies feelings of 'us and them' at a time when staffs need to pull together to cope with the turbulence of the schools environment.

5 The fact that most promotion is tied to taking on added administrative responsibility misleads staff at all levels, and has brought about a confusion between management and routine administration.

Departments and Department Heads

Despite all the problems in secondary schools, some are doing much better than others. This difference is even more marked at departmental level. The department is the unit with which staff members most naturally identify and this is where there is the greatest scope for effective management of the situation. Some departments are doing much better than others. How are these differences to be accounted for?

Differences between departments hinge mainly on the way the Head of Department interprets his or her role. The HoD is to the department what the Head is to the school: a major force for good or ill. The HoD's influence is rarely neutral, because of the position-power inherent in the role, and the expectations that this power gives rise to, and which must be met. Thus the HoD is either part of the problem or part of the solution. There can be no 'quick fix', but logically there are certain attitudes and behaviours which lead to a low quality department, and others which will tend to promote a higher quality contribution from staff.

1 Do you agree with that paragraph?
2 In what ways are you to the department what the Head is to the school?
3 In what ways can you *not* be to the department what the Head is to the school?
4 How do you think the members of your department see your role?

Despite the proliferation of pastoral systems and cross-curricular initiatives and faculty groupings, departments are still crucial to the pupil's success. This has been recognised by HMI: 'Whether a pupil achieves or underachieves is largely dependent on the quality of planning, execution, and evaluation that takes place within individual departments' (HMI Wales, 1984).

Some departments are little more than a collection of individuals who happen to teach the same subject in the same school. For a department to be something more than just the sum of its parts, it needs to function as a team. The contribution of all the members of the department needs to be mobilised if schools are to be able to adapt to the demands now being placed upon them. This can present considerable difficulties for the Head of Department and the other post-holders.

1 How should you interpret your role in what should be a team situation?
2 To what extent are you really 'in charge'?
3 How do you reconcile your own ideas with the expectations of your subordinates and superordinates?

This adds up to a classic middle management dilemma, which all Heads of Department need to confront on the way to building and then maintaining an effective department.

Two factors seem crucial for effectiveness:

1 Credibility

The Head of Department and the other post-holders must have credibility in the eyes of other departmental staff. (This is examined in more detail on pages 11–13.)

The following can be done as an individual exercise or as a group discussion activity:

1 Jot down briefly your ideas in response to this question:
   How can a Head of Department build and maintain credibility? What works best? What are the common pitfalls?

2 Read Document I: *Credibility*. How do your answers compare with the results of the survey? Do you agree with their views?

(About 45 minutes.)

2 Professional leadership and quality control

... the effectiveness of a school will continue to hinge in certain fundamental respects upon the competence of its heads of department, and the quality of professional leadership demanded for success at this level is higher than that implied by the modest status often accorded to heads of department in school hierarchies.

(Welsh Office, 1981)

The second crucial issue is what can loosely be termed quality control. Some make it sound very straightforward:

> Within a school or college superordinates have a right and an obligation to monitor and judge the performance of subordinates.
>
> (Lambert et al., 1985)

> Responsibilities of Heads of Department ... 10, regular review of teachers' record and mark books, 11, regular inspections of samples of work within the department.
>
> (*A Comprehensive School Staff Handbook*, 1987)

Ribbins (1985), on the other hand, indicates that in reality one of the major sources of criticism of Heads of Department lies exactly in their performance of their supervisory function.

> Many commentators emphasise the importance of control, supervision and the monitoring of the work of departmental staff as a key, even *the* key, function of the middle manager. ... This may well be correct, but it is almost equally widely recognised that this is an aspect of their work which causes many heads of department great role-strain ...
>
> In some cases inadequate action is the result of failure to appreciate the extent to which responsibilities have multiplied and increased in importance but this is often accompanied by a traditional reluctance to interfere with the professional work of one's colleagues. (p. 361)

Even conscientious Heads of Department feel that monitoring by classroom observation is still a very sensitive issue; similarly there is a clear danger that such a blatant exercise of authority as inspecting colleagues' record books and exercise books might well undermine good departmental relationships and other aspects of team-building. Such formal top-down mechanisms frequently do more harm than good.

Nevertheless, the aim of quality control is a valid one, and there is research evidence that subordinates in fact feel that their superiors *ought* to exercise their professional leadership by taking an interest in their work and they feel disappointed and undervalued when this does not happen. But how is this quality control best achieved?

The following can be done as an individual development task, but is probably most instructive when discussed as a group containing staff at different promotion levels!

1 Consider and note down ideas in response to this question:

> How can a busy Head of Department, usually working a full teaching timetable, best promote high quality work from the departmental staff? What works? What doesn't? How is it best monitored?

2 Read Document II: Quality control.
3 Compare your ideas.
4 Read Document III: Effective departments.

Consider the list of features. How can some of these ideas be put into practice? Select one or two for detailed exploration. Some can be developed, either alone or with other members of the department, using other exercises in this book.

Team management Document I: Credibility

For a department to be effective, the Head of Department needs to have credibility in the eyes of the other departmental staff. Three groups of staff were asked to consider how credibility could be gained, maintained or lost.

Group 1 reported:
Credibility is gained by:
- leading by example
- style of management of staff – firm and fair, but sensitive, respecting others' views
- knowledge of the subject
- belief in the value of the subject
- being prepared to stand up for the interests of the department and its members
- being interested in keeping up-to-date, and open to new ideas, but without necessarily climbing onto every bandwagon

Credibility can be lost by:
- lack of any of the above, in particular by being too autocratic

Group 2 reported:
Credibility is gained by:
- being a good teacher
- sharing the load of classes, rooms, and resources
- consistency, balanced by
- an openness to change

Credibility can be lost by:
- using the privilege of office to obtain unfair advantages, eg all the best classes

Group 3 reported:
Credibility is gained by:
- valuing the opinions and expertise of others in the department
- doing plenty of the 'dirty jobs'
- leading by example
- encouraging teamwork
- providing constant support and reassurance, without undermining
- being able to talk to people, being a good colleague

Credibility can be lost by:
- not delegating enough
- setting yourself up as perfect
- stifling the opinions of others
- consulting and then taking no notice

Team management Document II: Quality control

The second key issue in departmental management is what can loosely be termed *quality control*. Three groups of staff were invited to generate and discuss ideas on how a busy Head of Department can best promote high quality work from the departmental staff? What works? What doesn't? How is it best monitored?

Group 1 reported:
The Head of Department *encourages* high quality work from colleagues by:
- good relationships
- plenty of discussion, informal as well as formal
- leading by example
- mutual support and advice
- sharing and delegating

It is best *monitored* by:
- constant review and discussion of progress and problems, visiting each other's classrooms, occasional team teaching.

Group 2 reported:
The Head of Department *encourages* high quality work from colleagues by:
- respect for colleagues
- time for colleagues (but no mere sham consultation)
- empathy with colleagues
- willingness to share responsibility

It is best *monitored* by:
- encouraging a team approach, eg by sharing the preparation of materials

Group 3 reported:
The Head of Department *encourages* high quality work from colleagues by:
- encouraging teamwork
- matching roles to personalities
- playing to people's strengths
- encouraging and being open to others' ideas
- not having a blinkered approach
- being efficient, by prioritising tasks

It is best *monitored* by:
- creating a great deal of cooperation among all the departmental staff
- developing the 'social side' of the department

Team management Document III: Effective departments

No two departments are the same, but it is likely that a successful department will exhibit some, if not all, of the following features; for a department to succeed in all of these areas would necessitate a team of paragons led by a super-paragon! This is therefore not a prescription for success, more a checklist of areas to think about.

Leadership
- Post-holders take the strain, lead from the front
- Post-holders feel accountable downwards, as well as upwards
- All necessary team roles are fulfilled by someone, but not all by the Head of Department
- Appropriate loose-tight balance*
- Consious departmental culture and ethos, shared values and expectations
- High expectations – concern for quality continually emphasised

Relationships
- Cohesion – team spirit
- Coordination through scheme of work
- Collaboration in selection and preparation of materials
- Intensive informal interaction – plenty of 'talking shop'
- Sharing of problems and solutions
- Supporting each other
- Warmth and empathy, rather than professional distance and impersonality
- Openness – no taboo areas of discussion
- Atmosphere of trust – can cope with and deal with conflict, not suppress it
- Can all visit each other's teaching rooms

---

* 'Loose-tight balance' is an expression coined by Peters and Waterman in their influential study of effective companies *In Search of Excellence* (1984). What does the leader need to control, and what can be left to subordinates to do autonomously? Getting this right is the art of good management. For example: a department of inexperienced or not very competent staff will need a more rigid scheme of work and closer, more frequent support and monitoring than a department staffed with clearly creative, experienced and competent staff. Thus the style of leadership and the 'loose-tight balance' must fit the circumstances.

© Derek Torrington, Jane Weightman, Basil Blackwell Ltd, 1989.

- Sensitive monitoring
- Felt-fair shares of rooms, resources, classes

Beyond the department
- Good marketing of the department – cultivation of a departmental image
- Open to good ideas from outside
- Can generate change, sniff the wind, stay ahead of the trend
- Adept at acquiring resources in and out of school
- Careful recruitment (even head-hunting!) and induction

Section Two
STRUCTURED EXERCISES FOR GROUPS – INSET

This largest section of the book contains material which might be particularly suitable for use on days devoted to in-service training. All the material is designed for work in groups of varying size; trainers need to study the material for each chapter carefully before deciding how to use it – if at all. Chapters 7 and 13, for instance, can lead to quite searching discussion, with results that could be difficult to handle. This is not to suggest that the topics should be avoided, as they are fundamental and important, but the trainer will need to work out the most appropriate strategy and timing.

The exercises provided are:

6 Management and organisation in successful schools: prescription, leadership, collegiality or anarchy
   Structured analysis of school culture
7 Meetings: deciding the types of meeting to run
   Group discussion on the function of meetings
8 Meetings/mechanics: deciding how they should be run
   Group discussion on how to improve meetings
9 Job definition and individual feedback: how teachers know what their job is
   Group discussion on methods of management improvement
10 Appraisal: how teachers know how they are doing
   Introductory one-day training course in appraisal
11 Communications I: purposes and methods
   Structured analysis of school communication methods
12 Senior management teams: finding cohesion and purpose
   Weekend course for a school's senior team
13 Change
   Group discussion/role-playing on facilitating change

6 Management and organisation in successful schools: prescription, leadership, collegiality or anarchy

The first of our group INSET exercises draws participants into an examination of what lies at the heart of the way their school is organised. It is suitable for all members of teaching and non-teaching staff in groups of five upwards, but the trainer needs to work through the material very thoroughly in advance so as to be prepared for the searching discussion that is likely to ensue.

On completion of the exercise participants should be able to:

a) distinguish prescription, leadership, collegiality and anarchy as ways of managing and organising;
b) describe their own preferred style and that of their school;
c) discuss the advantages and disadvantages of each sort.

Participants will need:
MOSS Document I – *Individual questionnaire*
MOSS Document II – *School questionnaire*
MOSS Document III – *A blank grid*
MOSS Document IV – *The MOSS Quadrants*

Introduction

The quadrants model (see MOSS Document IV) was developed after our research in schools. It is particularly useful for introducing people to discussing management and organisation. Document IV gives the basis for a talk. This could be given before participants complete the questionnaires, or afterwards. The advantage of giving the questionnaires first is that participants do not know what answer they want to give; the difficulty is that the task can appear rather abstract.

Document I/Document II: The Questionnaires

1 Get each individual to fill in *Document I: Individual questionnaire*, based on their individual likes and dislikes. Each contrasted pair of

statements has a nine point scale between them. Participants draw round the appropriate number to suggest their opinion. For example:

I like chocolate   1   2   3   4   5   ⑥   7   8   9   I dislike chocolate

would suggest a moderate dislike of chocolate.
(About 20 minutes)
2 Get each individual to fill in *Document II: School questionnaire*, based on their perception of the methods prevailing in the school at the moment.
(20 minutes)
3 Score both questionnaires. (Note that the scales of 1–9 vary.)
4 Add the scores for questions 1, 3, 4, 6, 9 to give the *consensus/conflict* axis.
5 Add the scores for questions 2, 5, 7, 8, 10 to give the *control/autonomy* axis.
(10 minutes)

Document III: The blank grid

1 Get each person to place a mark to locate their combined scores on the grid: this shows their preferred management and organisation.
2 Get them to put another mark to indicate their score for their school.
(10 minutes)
3 Now lead a discussion comparing individuals' two scores and examining differences between individuals.

Points for discussion might be:
• Differences within the group over what is ideal
• Explanations for differences between ideal and reality
• Differences between individuals in view of reality
• When would the different quadrants be most appropriate?
• Have things changed?
• Are they changing?
• What about departments?

Conclusion

You might conclude by indicating the MOSS project conclusions that both dithering in the centre or going to the extremes has disadvantages.

Management and organisation Document I:
Individual questionnaire

Circle the number that represents your opinion or preference.

Tough competition between colleagues in an organisation may create distrust and hostility, but is needed to stimulate hard work.	9 8 7 6 5 4 3 2 1	A strong sense of teamwork and support in the organisation is most likely to produce good results.
People at work should have considerable freedom to decide their own activities, collaborating with colleagues in any way they wish.	1 2 3 4 5 6 7 8 9	Activities should be closely controlled from the centre, with little individual decision making and few personal initiatives.
It is a good idea to ask for help from colleagues, as they have resources to share.	1 2 3 4 5 6 7 8 9	One should be cautious about seeking help from colleagues, as they may take advantage.
There are a few colleagues with whom one could share hopes and discuss career plans.	9 8 7 6 5 4 3 2 1	One could feel confident about sharing hopes and career plans with most of one's colleagues.
Duties are precisely set down for me by someone else, with little scope for personal initiative.	9 8 7 6 5 4 3 2 1	As far as possible people plan their own work and take considerable personal initiative.
All members of the organisation should support, and agree with, the organisation's objectives.	1 2 3 4 5 6 7 8 9	It doesn't matter whether or not all members of the organisation agree with its objectives, as long as they do a good job.
Financial expenditure should be tightly controlled by top managers.	9 8 7 6 5 4 3 2 1	Financial controls should be loose enough for people to plan their own expenditure.
Policy and strategy for the organisation is decided by top managers only.	9 8 7 6 5 4 3 2 1	Policy and strategy for the organisation should be decided by extensive consultation with all members.
When there is a problem all should join in to find a solution.	1 2 3 4 5 6 7 8 9	When there is a problem, it should be resolved by the person responsible.
Arrangements for time off and other absence should be made according to strict rules.	9 8 7 6 5 4 3 2 1	There should be individual freedom to take time off work in a responsible way, according to personal needs.

Management and organisation Document II:
School questionnaire

There is much conflict of interest, creating distrust and hostility.	9 8 7 6 5 4 3 2 1	There is complete harmony of interest in the organisation, with a strong sense of teamwork and mutual support.
We all enjoy considerable freedom to decide our own activities, collaborating with colleagues in any way we wish.	1 2 3 4 5 6 7 8 9	We are closely controlled from the centre, with little scope for individual decision making and no encouragement to take initiatives with colleagues.
I can rely on colleagues to help me.	1 2 3 4 5 6 7 8 9	I am afraid to ask for help from my colleagues.
There are a number of my colleagues with whom I would not share my hopes and career plans.	9 8 7 6 5 4 3 2 1	I would feel confident about discussing my hopes and career plans with most of my colleagues.
My duties are precisely set down for me by someone else, with little scope for personal initiative.	9 8 7 6 5 4 3 2 1	As far as possible people plan their own work and take considerable personal initiative.
We all agree with, and support, the organisation's objectives	1 2 3 4 5 6 7 8 9	We have different ideas about what we are trying to do.
Financial expenditure is tightly controlled by top managers.	9 8 7 6 5 4 3 2 1	We all have some money to spend how we like.
Policy and strategy for the organisation is decided by top management only.	9 8 7 6 5 4 3 2 1	We have extensive consultation and participation in policy decisions.
When there is a problem we all join in to find a solution.	1 2 3 4 5 6 7 8 9	When there is a problem the people responsible resolve it.
Arrangements for time off and other absence are made according to strict rules.	9 8 7 6 5 4 3 2 1	We take time off work when we need it.

Management and organisation Document III: Blank grid

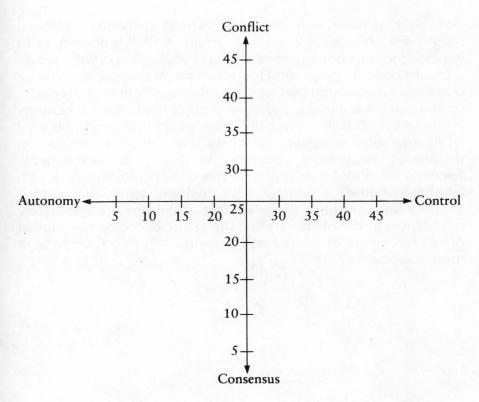

Management and organisation Document IV:
The MOSS Quadrants

Schools that cope well with their various demands and challenges are not always similar. A model we have developed to explore the tensions of managing and organising within secondary schools is given in Figure 1. The horizontal dimension represents the tension between the degree of tight central control on the one hand and the degree of group or individual autonomy on the other. This illustrates the range of ways that schools deal with, and who decides, such *structural* things as resources, finance, timetables, curriculum, staffing, job descriptions, teaching methodologies and schemes of work. A school in which all these matters are dealt with centrally would be located towards the right hand side, but that could move progressively left as the number of matters and the nature of choice was moved out of the hands of the few at the centre and into the hands of more members of staff.

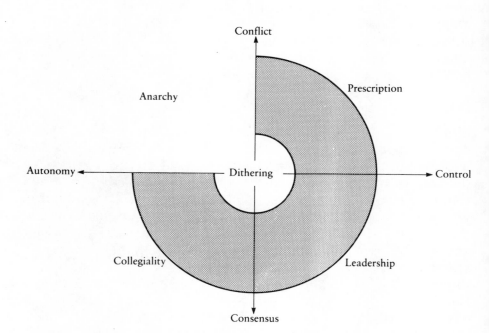

Figure 1 Effective managment can be found in any of the shaded areas.

© Derek Torrington, Jane Weightman, Basil Blackwell Ltd, 1989.

The vertical dimension represents a different tension, between values of consensus and relationships of high trust at one extreme, contrasted with low trust and conflicting interests at the other. This tells us something about the *culture* of the school and represents both the assumptions people make and the behaviour in which they engage. If a significant number of people, or a small number with significant power, believe the school to be staffed by members of different groups whose interests conflict, then they will also believe that the main management and organisation task is to deal with this conflict and their behaviour will reflect that belief. If the prevailing belief is that there are teams within the school who work together to the same ends, with the management and organisation task being to nurture this consensus, then behaviour will follow that assumption.

Putting these two dimensions together produces four quadrants labelled prescription, leadership, collegiality and anarchy, which represent the dominant management and organisational style operating. The prescription style is likely where there is a felt need for a lot of control mechanisms to manage the conflict within the school; the leadership style is more likely when a similar felt need to control is linked with a strong consensus supporting the initiatives of the senior management team. Although we find it difficult to recommend the anarchic style for any normal school situation, each of the other three styles has both advantages and disadvantages.

Prescription

The prescription style imposes order and allows for a lot of co-ordination, with little duplication of effort; resources are allocated on a rational basis. Prescription is most appropriate for dealing with matters that are routine and predictable. Such things as how to conduct fire drills and what to do about children who come late are best dealt with by clear, laid-down procedures; otherwise time is wasted and effort expended where it should not be needed. In one school, for example, there was no standard drill for the simple, routine task of collecting the registers, so that no-one knew what to do and one of the Deputy Heads spent half an hour each day re-inventing how to do it, asking for information and checking what was happening.

Prescription can also be appropriate when there is a major crisis or when the identity of the school is unclear, as in the amalgamation of two or more schools during re-organisation. All organisations need some co-ordination, predictability and control: prescription is appropriate to achieve these ends when other methods have failed, are too time-consuming or are difficult to achieve because of temporary staffing. When a school has had a strong leader as Head, the prescription style can be appropriate in the aftermath, as it provides an alternative structure after the collapse of the spider's web, woven by the departed Head.

As a general approach to running the school, prescription can thus be appropriate for a number of temporary situations. The difficulty is to find a way of moving to some other approach to ensure the school is flexible enough to cope with changing demands. Prescribing the right things but holding back from prescribing how people should teach is a very difficult balance to achieve. In its most benign form, prescription cleans up the administrative detail and minimises the routine frustrations of organisational life. It enables things to happen by removing impediments but it generates no excitement, raises no enthusiasm and makes no contribution to creativity.

There are some signs that prescription is becoming the new orthodoxy in school management. This perhaps stems from a vain hope that the world can be made stable by procedures and systems. However, the current and impending innovation overload for schools is such that there are many things that will be unpredictable and which need managing in other ways than by prescription.

Leadership

The leadership style can promote a sense of purpose and mission, with effort contributed willingly to this end; staff often feel valued personally and feel secure as they look up to the leader. Leadership seems particularly appropriate at the two extremes of experience: in a very stable environment and in very turbulent, life-threatening times. In stable times a leader can make control more acceptable by being a good communicator and can humanise the structures and procedures. In turbulent times, such as amalgamation, losing the Sixth Form, or poor press reports, a strong leader can embody what needs to be done and so help in the business of creating the new purpose. The difficulty is that the strong leader so embodies the unity of the school that it becomes almost a theological heresy to attack the leader. Flexibility, as well as uncertainty, is reduced. Not only does everyone follow the leader, they also wait for the leader and are inhibited from suggesting an appropriate route to follow.

Collegiality

The collegiality style emphasises collaboration and team work, enabling each member to contribute more. Methodologies and styles appropriate to different needs can be used; flexibility to meet new demands is easier to achieve and individuals can feel valued members of the school. Collegiality is in many ways the opposite of prescription. It is particularly appropriate for dealing with technical matters such as how and what to teach, to whom. It is needed in situations where a staff contribution that goes beyond simple compliance with instructions is required, as the person in charge can perhaps specify *what* is to be done ('More imaginative teaching of French, please') but can rarely specify *how* the goal is to be reached. Collegiality is the better way of managing and organising in novel situations where no-one is quite sure what the required performance actually is, such as the introduction of GCSE, or the national curriculum, where each individual teacher has to make it happen.

Collegiality has such an obvious appeal that it is tempting to regard it as the 'best way' to run a school. However, where there is a shortage of competent people, a high percentage of temporary staff, a high turnover of staff, a lot of inexperienced staff or conflicting loyalties, the school will be poorly served by collegial managing and organising. It is a flexible way of organising where there is sufficient stability of personnel for continuity.

Anarchy

The anarchy style seeks to meet the ideal of individual rights to self-expression and development of potential free from the constraints of control mechanisms or the discipline of conforming to group norms. We had no examples of this type of school in our sample. It is associated with such schools as Summerhill, Dartington and William Tyndale, but each of these had a strong leader as founding father. The disadvantage of this style is persuading others that this individuality is what schools should be about.

So what would MOSS recommend? We contend that none of the styles can be pursued to its extreme without creating serious organisational difficulties. Equally, we would argue that dithering in the centre with no clear view leads to loss of identity, direction and confidence. Each of the three main styles is appropriate for particular situations. Prescription is appropriate where consistency is important. Leadership is helpful when there is uncertainty that can and should be dealt with quickly. Collegiality is useful when the full commitment of individuals is necessary. All schools have all these in different proportions at different times. The balance between them is the clever art of finding the appropriate management and organisation for the particular school.

7 Meetings: deciding the types of meeting to run

This book includes a great deal of material about communications, especially meetings. We have presented this material in a sequence which seems logical, but individual trainers will need to decide what is relevant to their own situation. We suggest the material in this first communications chapter is suitable in a school where radical change in meeting arrangements is being considered.

On completion members of the group should be able to:

a) fit each of the meetings in their school into one of the suggested categories;
b) understand the advantages and disadvantages of each type of meeting;
c) decide whether the meeting should be continued, reconstituted or scrapped.

Participants will need:
Meetings Document I – *Types of meeting*

To the trainer

This exercise should take about two hours. It starts from the assumption that most teachers feel they have a lot of meetings. To decide whether they are all necessary we need first to ask what function each meeting serves. The purpose of this exercise is to review the different types of meeting held within participants' own school, using a set of categories derived from the MOSS research.

Introduction

Present the analysis (below) of the ways in which meetings differ. This presentation should take 20 to 25 minutes, followed by 20 minutes discussion.

The MOSS research found the following types of meeting in the schools studied:

Whole staff meetings may take various forms:

- The traditional *general staff meeting* is usually held once or twice a term, although in some schools it has been discontinued due to the introduction of meetings with a more specific focus.
- *Briefing meetings* are held weekly or daily. They last only a few minutes, and are mainly for providing information rather than for discussion.
- *INSET* often takes the form of a meeting for all staff to deal with an issue of general interest.
- *Ad hoc meetings* may be called to deal with a particular matter that has cropped up: so that all staff can be informed of the development; to sound out opinion; or to ensure broad support for a proposed course of action.

Vertical slice meetings are where a group meets to deal with matters which affect people at different levels in the hierarchy, but narrowly rather than broadly. The main examples are the meetings of a *department, faculty, year* or *house*, to deal with matters that do not concern those with other specialist interests.

Horizontal slice meetings are of people with similar levels of responsibility across the school. *Senior staff, Heads of Department and Heads of Year* meetings are the most obvious examples, as people meet to find common ground and co-ordinate action to resolve issues that affect all, or a number, of the school's departments.

Expertise or interest meetings occur where a group or working party sets out to tackle a particular topic that potentially involves staff across the school and where working out of ideas is needed before progress can be made. Membership of the groups is likely to be on the basis of particular staff expertise, or on the basis of picking those interested in the topic. The group membership does not coincide with the established groupings in the school (department, year and so forth) and the effectiveness of their deliberations can be hampered by that indeterminate status.

Interface meetings take place at the school boundary, for example case conferences or TVEI meetings with members of the local college. These meetings cause few problems. Partly this is due to the technical nature of the work that is being undertaken, but also the involvement of outsiders tends to draw the school staff members together.

Points for discussion:

1 *How would you expect the approach to running these various types of meeting to differ?*

Draw out especially comments on:

- the special skill needed to deal with large meetings, where there is a diversity of interests and a number of different points of view;
- the relative ease of interface meetings because of interpersonal rivalries or antagonisms being suppressed;
- the need for expertise or interest meetings to have a clear brief so that the enthusiasm of members does not turn sour;
- the difference of attitude to be expected in vertical and horizontal slice meetings and how these differences are to be handled;
- the need to limit discussion in briefing meetings.

2 *Have you personal experience of a meeting that is of the wrong type to achieve its objectives?*
Expect comments on:

- whole-staff meetings grappling with detail, when a report from a working party could have presented proposals for acceptance with minor modifications;
- 'slice' meetings where the slice is too thick or too thin;
- briefing meetings that repeat information already supplied.

There will be other points, but avoid too many favourite horror stories that have no useful message.

Document I: Types of meeting

Document I contains samples of five different types of meeting. Distribute a copy to all participants and take the samples one at a time. Allow a few minutes to read each one before moving to the points for discussion. Samples 1, 3 and 4 require more discussion than sample 2. Sample 5 is merely an illustration. Allow no more than 30 to 40 minutes; otherwise the discussion will become repetitive.

The following findings from the MOSS research may help the discussion:

1 Staff members generally found *general staff meetings* unsatisfactory. This was largely due to the number of people present and consequent unwieldiness as a means of discussion or questioning for clarification. Many Heads (who nearly always chaired such meetings) obviously found the occasions difficult to handle and some regarded the processes of such meetings as destructive of their authority. When observing general staff meetings, we often found that there was poor preparation and preliminary information, so that staff attended without any readiness for the matters to be addressed and without any apparent will to make the meeting succeed. The Head then had

to work hard to win them round, and seldom succeeded in overcoming that initial disadvantage.

General staff meetings were more likely to be successful when there was a published agenda (perhaps with briefing notes available beforehand), preparation by those involved in initiating discussion, and a setting that did not unwittingly cast the staff in the role of children sitting at desks and being 'taught' from the front.

2 *Departmental meetings* posed few problems for staff except in those cases where there was an unpopular or incompetent Head of Department. Where meetings were informal and frequent, there was the great advantage that subject specialism gave all participants a common language and set of assumptions that made communication relatively easy and helped the process of group solidarity. A further advantage was that these meetings often had to resolve issues that did not involve individual status, career prospects or deeply-held conviction. Deciding whether to use *Zigger-Zagger* or *The Merchant of Venice* is infinitely easier than resolving whether or not children should wear school uniform.

For general departmental co-ordination and smoothness of operation, some Heads of Department were developing manuals for the guidance of subject specialists. These combined a sequence for teaching the subject year by year, together with lists of materials available, standard letters to send to parents and so forth. Although didactic in tone, these manuals were welcomed by individual staff members, especially as they included some type of contribution from everyone at some point. Heads of Department were readily granted considerable authority where others had the feeling of having contributed their portion. The manuals were akin to the minutes of a hundred mini-meetings: the informality and ease of the meetings both permitting and creating the authority of the manual, which gradually became the central organising feature of the department.

3 *Year and House meetings* were less frequent, partly because they involved more people and partly because of the difficulty in going across departments on the timetable whilst industrial action was either recent or present. In one or two instances Year/House groupings were used to get staff views on cross-school issues that were not strictly pastoral. One school, for example, got staff views on the new curriculum statement in House meetings convened during assembly time.

4 *Heads of Department/Faculty meetings* were seen in many schools as a major power centre. Indeed, in one instance the Headteacher muscled in on this meeting during our stay, having realised how powerful it was. Since then he has either gone himself or sent one of his deputies. This type of meeting is often chaired by different

members of the group on a rotational basis.

5 *Heads of Year/House meetings* tended to be mutual support sessions focusing on co-ordinating activities, usually chaired by the Deputy Head in charge of pastoral matters.

6 *Working parties* are an easy way of avoiding an issue in the short-term. When debate at the whole staff meeting is becoming heated and there is no apparent solution to a knotty problem, setting up a working party defuses the situation and gives hope for a satisfactory outcome eventually. The main difficulties are that group members may be a mis-match, chosen more to neutralise their potential for disagreement than for their ability to contribute, and that they are not clear of their terms of reference. Skilled and experienced members of staff will find their way round those problems, but their prospects are improved if they receive a reasonably clear brief on how far they can go and what they are expected to achieve.

Our observation of working parties found some to be well-run with enthusiastic participation generating useful output. But many showed signs of considerable frustration among participants, and some were clearly causing mistrust and harm to the ethos of the school.

Difficulties often stem from the ill-considered way in which the working party was set up. Among the cynical aphorisms from management folklore are: 'When in doubt set up a working party . . .' and 'Decision-making too easily degenerates into a call for further analysis'.

How to get the right types of meeting

Allow 30 minutes for this part of the exercise. Ask group members to draw up a personal, or collective, action plan for their own situation around the following suggestions:

1 Only convene a meeting or set up a working party if it is necessary; not as a solution to some other problem.

2 Review the regular meetings that are held now. Are they all correctly constituted for the purposes they serve? Are whole staff meetings dealing with matters better handled by vertical or horizontal slice groupings? Are horizontal slice meetings dealing with matters that should be handled in vertical slice groupings, or vice versa? Can any meetings be amalgamated? Should any meetings be wound up with their work being taken on by an individual? Are there matters being dealt with by individuals that should be remitted to meetings?

3 Review the working parties currently operating. How many are operating effectively? Do the others have a clear brief? Are the matters being investigated suitable for working party study? How and when do they report their findings? When was the last ineffective working party? Why did it not succeed? Will that problem recur?

Meetings Document I: Types of meeting

1 Whole staff – A staff meeting at Kirkside

This was the first staff meeting for two years and was attended by 37 staff. There was a published agenda and minutes were taken by the Commerce teacher.

All the agenda items were introduced by the Head and he allowed discussion to take place. He appeared ill-at-ease, almost as if he was scared of meetings; this was exploited by the more vociferous staff, so that the meeting appeared almost to get out of control. Some tension was displayed; one of the most senior of the teachers seemed particularly negative and argumentative, lounging back with his feet on the table and losing no opportunity to be critical of the Head and of his own colleagues. He is, with some justification, known as 'the leader of the opposition' by the Head. Two other senior members of staff showed a degree of petulance and an aggressiveness towards their more junior colleagues, and two Heads of Department spent most of the time muttering to each other without making any positive contribution to the meeting. The senior teacher was subjected to vindictive comments over profiling, probably because of the animosity felt in some quarters regarding her appointment.

Points for discussion:
- What harm is this meeting doing?
- Could the problems have been avoided?
- What can be done now?

2 Vertical slice – A Humanities Faculty meeting at Westcliffe

For three consecutive Wednesdays, six members of this Faculty met to discuss the content and methodology of the second year programme. The membership consisted of all those who taught this year and included a Deputy, the Head of Faculty, Head of History, an experienced Scale 1 teacher, a young Scale 2 teacher and a Scale 2 teacher who had been redeployed from teaching Office Practice. The discussion centred on integrating History, RE and Geography and whether a sequential or thematic approach should be taken. Everyone took part, voicing different views. The Head of Faculty chaired the meeting, as he was the only one not teaching the year.

Points for discussion
- What makes the meeting topic suitable for vertical slice approach?
- Is the membership appropriate?

3 Horizontal slice – A Year Heads' meeting at Southern High

At the start of the meeting only Mr H, Mr P, and Mr M were present. Mr B came in five minutes later and Miss C 15 minutes later.

Matters arising from the minutes – Mr H said that despite the minutes having been put out to all staff, he had had only one reaction.

He reported that he had attended the working party on school rules and uniform, the minutes of which had been just put out by Mr M. He was pleased to see that the working party was in favour of the retention of uniform. All three Year Heads reaffirmed their own stance in favour of the retention of uniform. They discussed the importance of their interests and views as Year Heads being represented on such working parties. They as a group wish to be able to influence decisions.

There was some discussion of the consequences of abolishing corporal punishment. Mr B believed that although corporal punishment was now used very little within the school, its formal abolition would lead to greater use of suspension procedures, greater liaison with parents and, therefore, even greater calls on the time of the Year Head.

Even now, said Mr B (reiterating what he had already said in the full staff meeting), pastoral work was eating into lesson time. Mr M agreed and said that this should not be hidden from staff: it was a fact of life. For example, if a parent arrives without an appointment on a matter of some urgency, you have to see them. They discussed this further and agreed that they should ask for more non-teaching periods – at least one per day, and particularly one before break on a Monday morning.

They discussed the fact that last year the roles of the Deputies had been changed; they no longer had any pastoral responsibility for Upper or Lower School. Responsibility for serious referrals now lay with Mr H and Mr M. They were conscious of certain anxieties among the staff about not having a Pastoral Deputy to refer to. They discussed whether there was any danger of the ordinary Year Heads being by-passed now and staff going straight to Mr M or Mr H as the senior tutors. Mr M thought not.

© Derek Torrington, Jane Weightman, Basil Blackwell Ltd, 1989.

Point for discussion:
● What makes this meeting so negative?

4 Expertise or interest – A working party on discipline at Renold

This was one of two working parties set up by the Head. In his paper to the staff he states:

'The group is to consider the implications of HMI comments with regard to:
1 Staff/pupil relationships
2 Attitudes and expectations – of staff towards pupils and to each other and of pupils to staff and to each other, and is to make recommendations for changes in classroom approaches or methodology that would lead to improvements as defined by the group with regard to relationships and attitudes'.

The group is chaired by the Head of Special Needs, and she has overall responsibility for its composition. Some staff were nominated by the Head but others volunteered to become involved. Initially, it contained ten members but not all staff were able to go to the meetings. The group works to an agenda and minutes are available to all staff.

It was decided to attempt to get all staff involved and questionnaires were sent out, of which 78% were returned.

26 members of staff agreed to attend fortnightly meetings this term. These were divided into three groups and further subdivided into two for detailed discussion. The sub-groups were all led by a member of the working party. It was planned that each group would meet five times during the term, 15 meetings altogether.

The method adopted was for a problem to be set for initial response by the 26 members of staff. These responses were shared in meetings of the sub-groups before full discussion with all participants. After that there would be recommendations on action or requests for further discussion.

We attended a group meeting at which ten members of staff were present. They all took the exercise seriously and there was a very valuable exchange of views and experiences to which everybody contributed. The aim was to consider personal views of disruption and to try to identify common factors.

When all the group meetings have taken place, the working party will meet again and will report to the Headteacher.

The Headteacher and Deputy Headteacher were specifically

excluded from the initial meetings because the working party leader felt that their presence would inhibit discussion.

Eventually it is hoped that the school will develop its own material (at present it is using a published pack) and the indications are that the progress made by the team will make a real contribution to staff development in the school.

Points for discussion:
- Is the membership of the working party appropriate?
- Are there useful by-products of this process apart from finding solutions to the problems of discipline?

5 Interface meeting – A Hall End case conference

The Head of Lower School has a weekly case conference with the educational psychologist, EWO, Social Services and the Head of the attached hostel. They run for two hours and the Heads of Years 1, 2 and 3 come in succession when pupils in their year are being discussed. An agenda and minutes are presented, with the children only referred to by case number. In the space of two hours a rapid review of each child is given. Discussion focuses on new or difficult cases and the action required by the various services.

Points for discussion:
- Is it appropriate for the Heads of Year to come in succession?
- How useful are minutes referred to by number?

8 Meetings/mechanics: deciding how they should be run

Having worked out the type of meetings that need to be run, we now move on to aspects of mechanics: how meetings are conducted. The materials consist of a series of topics for group discussion, starting with the experience of group members themselves, moving on to consider a range of situations in other schools and finishing with a checklist. Group sizes could range from 5–25.

On completion members of the group should be able to:

a) understand the main aspects of administration and procedure that will make a meeting successful;
b) agree outline methods of procedure and administration likely to make their own meetings successful.

Participants will need:
Meetings/mechanics Document I – *The Fifth Year Form Teachers' Meeting*
Meetings/mechanics Document II – *Further meeting problems*
Meetings/mechanics Document III – *The checklist.*

To the trainer

This exercise is timed to take approximately three hours. It is appropriate for staff at all levels in the school, not just those who have to lead or chair meetings. It can be conducted with groups ranging in size from five or six to 20+. Participants should have a common interest in meetings that will focus their analysis and help in developing norms and procedures that are relevant to their particular situation. All the members of a department or faculty would be one such grouping.

For a meeting to be a success, it is not sufficient just to know *why* it is being held; the *processes* by which a meeting works have to be understood as well. In the MOSS Project, 433 meetings were observed. In many, the participants exhibited such a limited understanding of the basic mechanics of meetings that there was inadequate discussion, understanding and action about important matters. Poor meetings not only fail to achieve objectives; they can also do harm, as members become frustrated about lack of progress or about not being able to get their point of view across. It is not just the fault of the person in charge: all participants have to learn meeting mechanics. The analogy of the orchestra is apt. The conductor is responsible for the final quality of the co-ordinated act, but every instrumentalist has to make a distinctive – but not individualistic – contribution that blends with all the others.

Some very good practice was also observed in the schools.

Introduction

Ask groups to discuss the following questions:

1 *At a recent meeting you attended, what were the most obvious impediments to constructive discussion and subsequent action?* For example: one or two people talking too much, some making no contribution, poor agenda, no agenda, too much talking and too little listening, poor chairing. (Points like this need to be 'played back' for further discussion, such as 'What was wrong with the chairing of the meeting?')

2 *What caused these impediments?* Encourage members of the group to work out not just their complaints, but also an understanding of causes. For example, 'Did the people who talked too much do so because they thought it was expected of them? Because they always talk too much? Because they did not understand what was happening? Some other reason?'

3 *How could the problems have been overcome?* Aim here to get practical suggestions rather than general beliefs that things should be better. Suggestions about how they *personally* could have done something different are the most useful and worth developing. (10–20 minutes)

Now move the group on to consider the case of the Fifth Year Meeting (Document I).

Document I: The Fifth Year Form Teachers' Meeting

Group members should have copies of Meetings Document I *before* the training session.

Generate discussion of the various points at the end of the case (15 to 20 minutes in total).

The lessons to be drawn out from this case are mainly:

1 Much can be improved by careful attention to the details of running the meeting. Good intentions and the importance of the matter to be considered are not enough on their own.
2 Improving meeting administration cannot, however, compensate for other inadequacies in the way the school is run. Meetings do not constitute management; they are merely a part of the process.
3 The person in charge of the meeting takes the blame for things not being right. Those who feel overlooked or outmanoeuvred are merciless with those who have overlooked them – however unintentionally.
4 Mr S may have been very uncomfortable and may have lost respect in the eyes of his colleagues, but something has still been achieved: catharsis for group members and some information exchange.
5 All meetings have potential problems of discussion that cannot be handled because of lack of information at the time, or because the matter is simply too difficult. (This is sometimes known as 'opening a can of worms'.)

Document II: Further meeting problems

Distribute Document II. Allow participants five minutes to read each mini-case, followed by 10–15 minutes discussion of each.

The main lessons to draw out are:

1 **Francis Bacon** – the advantages of clear format, purpose and preparation, with the leader being in control. Year Heads were concentrating on *content* (passing on what the Head had said) but forgetting *process* (the way the meeting had been conducted). People will only attend and make a success of meetings they see as useful.
2 **Westcliffe** – few people are accustomed to expressing a point of view in a meeting and many find it inhibiting. Most people speak best when asked to and when speaking on something about which they are knowledgeable.

Leaders of meetings get contributions by asking people to speak, picking up non-verbal cues indicating a desire to speak or reaction to what someone else has said. Statements of fact rather than expressions of opinion are the easiest way for people to make their first contribution.

Experienced members of groups can help the less experienced by 'shaping' the clumsy or over-emotional comments of their colleagues and agreeing with them (for example: 'I would like to agree with what Hilary was saying and make the further point . . .' NOT 'I think Hilary was trying to say . . .').

3 **Summerfield High** – constantly emphasising the limited time available makes it harder for people to make coherent contributions. People speak more effectively and come to the point more quickly when not under time pressure.

It is better to get clear and effective action on one point than vague, incomplete decisions on three.

Brief, written notes of decisions, produced quickly, are the most effective way of tying down a decision. Memory begins to fade as soon as the meeting finishes, and before long each participant will have a different recollection of what was agreed.

Document III: The checklist

Distribute Document III and work through it with the group, encouraging members to modify the list in the light of their own situation. (Allow 30 minutes for this part of the exercise.)

Conclusion

1 Review the various phases of the exercise and ask each group member to produce a list of five main lessons learned. Compare notes. (30 minutes)
2 Ask each group member to produce an action plan of three things they will do differently about meetings in the future. Compare notes. (30 minutes)
3 The numbers of five and three are suggested in order to focus members' minds and make some follow-up action more likely. It is important that all members should produce action plans, not just those who actually run meetings. The effectiveness of the meeting depends on all participants.

Meetings/mechanics Document I:
The Fifth Year Form Teachers' Meeting

The Fifth Year Form Teachers' Meeting at Central High was scheduled to begin at 8.55 according to the school bulletin, which was the only announcement of the meeting. There was no reminder on the board in the staff workroom. At 9.05 staff were still drifting in to the classroom where the meeting was held. The idea seemed good; the bulletin said that the pupils were to go straight to assembly where they would be registered, so that the meeting could get off to a prompt start. For whatever reasons, it did not work out that way. Possibly the staff have become so used to meetings starting late that hardly anyone seems to consider it important to make an effort to arrive on time.

Just after 9.05 Mr S (Head of Upper School) said that he would just hang on a couple more minutes for the others to arrive. Meanwhile, he discussed a detail of the Chemistry examination entries with Mr H. At 9.06 Mr S decided to start the meeting. At this point, two people were still missing. Mr S started by announcing that he had now received copies of various external examination timetables. He asked Mr B what arrangements had been made the previous year for distributing timetables to the fifth year pupils. Mr S said that he would now give them reports from the various pastoral meetings held over the last few weeks.

The first item he reported was the role of the form teacher, which was mentioned as an agenda item on the Pastoral Admin meeting minutes that he was using as the basis of his report. He gave the impression that a working party on this had been set up and had reported to the Pastoral Admin meeting. There is indeed an intention to set up such a working party, but it has not yet been convened.

Mr S was immediately bombarded by questions arising from this piece of misinformation. Who was on this working party? Had membership on it been advertised? No-one had seen any notices about it – when had it met? etc. Mr S was unable to give satisfactory answers to any of these questions about a fictitious working party. The consensus which indignantly emerged was that any working party on the role of the form teacher needed some form teacher input and there was a suggestion that one form teacher should be elected from each year on to the working party. The contributions were vehement and articulate and it was some minutes before Mr S was able to get a word in. It was noticeable that the contributions came mainly from the experienced middle management present. Mr S finally got a word in. He said that he did not know as much about it as he should because he had been unable to attend more than one meeting, but he would investigate.

Mr S then reported on other, less controversial items, most of which the form teachers knew already, until he reached the item on the decision to set up a Pupils' Council. This again aroused a lot of very animated discussion, mainly from the group identified above, plus Mrs T – who is very articulate, has firm views, and is not afraid to express them. What was the Pupil Council for? What were its powers? What was its brief? Was it just going to be like the last one some years ago where the pupils made suggestions which were usually knocked on the head? Why the proposed structure? What does 'in school time' mean? This was followed by a series of opinions and suggestions: to get the best out of it, the children will need training in the workings of committees, the whole idea is artificial, a complicated formal structure will put people off, in school time is a good idea, encouraging greater participation, but what is it for?

Once again, Mr S found it difficult to get a word in and was able to contribute only because some of the comments from the others were framed as questions. At one point he felt impelled to interrupt Mrs T to attempt to explain its intended working. The discussion ranged on to what *used* to happen, how the sixth form used to be more involved with the other pupils and one or two contributions of the 'It's symptomatic' variety. Eventually, when the others seemed to have run out of steam, Mr S closed the discussion with 'I'll just write that down'. It was not clear just what he was writing down; it was probably based on Mrs T's extensive contribution, rather than the meeting as a whole. There was, in fact, no attempt to articulate a consensus (eg Are we agreed then that . . . Have I got this right . . .?).

The next item Mr S reported on was winter uniform, which seemed to be another old favourite, to judge by the reactions. 'It's a cop-out', 'How do other schools cope without lockers?', 'Get rid of bags and you get rid of a lot of the problems'.

Then the meeting ran out of time and Mr S asked members to think about pierced ears and attendance for next time.

Points for discussion:
- What prevented this meeting from being more successful?
- Which of those reasons was connected with the conduct of the meeting and which can be attributed to other aspects of the way the school was run?
- What mistakes did Mr S make and how could he have prevented them?
- Despite apparent difficulties, what *has* the meeting achieved?
- Has any harm been done? If so, what?

Meetings/mechanics Document II: Further meeting problems

1 Francis Bacon: a contrast of styles

The school senior management runs morning meetings with clear procedures and an opportunity for all to contribute. The meeting is held in the conference room; the Head gives a brief account of events for each day and uses the occasion to set the tone, or highlight things which need attention. He always goes round the table and invites colleagues, including the Deputy Heads and six Pastoral Heads, to contribute to the meeting. The deputy in charge of cover has a photocopied sheet which she makes available to each member of the meeting. The format is clear – for example, members of the meeting sit around a long table with diaries in front of them – and the form is open.

These meetings are followed, on two out of five days in each week, by 'cascaded' meetings of tutors. The Year Heads, who have just been with the Head, sit in a classroom or tutor room and, leading their pastoral colleagues, go over the same ground covered in the meeting held ten minutes before. Most of the six meeting formats we observed were considerably inferior to the first meetings. Staff did not sit around a table and often people arrived late or missed the meeting altogether. Few had paper or diaries to make notes on; the meeting leaders never gave their colleagues an opportunity to contribute in the way in which they had been invited to contribute at the first meetings and there was little evidence that they had thought through the type of meeting they were holding. Not surprisingly, the people who attended these meetings saw little point in them and several strongly resented the imposition they saw them as being. Whilst we were in the school the staff successfully had the five-meetings-a-week system reduced to two: some would have abolished the second meetings altogether.

Points for discussion:
- Why were the first level meetings more effective than those at the second level?
- List the aspects of meeting mechanics that the leaders of second level meetings could have introduced to improve the quality of their meetings.

Westcliffe: the problem of balanced contribution

The Humanities Faculty were having weekly meetings to re-design the second year syllabus. Many junior members of staff had difficulty in participating because they did not know how to present their case. This varied with faculty but the Humanities Faculty meetings observed showed that individuals with ideas to contribute did not get an adequate hearing: because they were outmanoeuvred by others; they presented their case too emotionally and only once, having had 'to get so much steam up' to get the confidence to speak in the first place. Senior members did not always help juniors to make contributions.

Points for discussion:
- What would enable junior members of staff to make their case more effectively in meetings?
- List ways in which the leader of the meeting could get better contribution from all members.
- List ways in which more senior members of the meeting could help others make their contribution.

Summerfield High: time, papers and minutes

In several meetings discussion of a topic was brief because of pressure of time – they used a 4.30 guillotine. Consequently many decisions were not tied down. This was exaggerated by the behaviour of the Headteacher who was constantly saying 'aware of time', 'I welcome that', 'We are aware of . . .', 'could do . . .', ie they were not tying down decisions and actions. Surprisingly, notes/minutes were not taken in these meetings by participants, although they were taken for curriculum planning meetings.

On several occasions documents were presented *at* the meeting, not before, with people being asked for immediate comments.

Points for discussion:
- What are the effects on discussion of a meeting guillotine?
- How can decisions and actions be tied down?

Meetings/mechanics Document III: The checklist

The following checklist of questions can be used both in making the arrangements for a regular meeting, or for planning a particular meeting session.

1 Who has the right to attend?
Particular job holders?
Their representatives?
Anyone, so that no one feels excluded?
....
....

2 What should the group consist of?
All those with the slightest interest including non-teaching staff?
A smaller group, to make discussion easier and more productive?
Representatives of each layer in the hierarchy?
A variety of personalities to ensure a lively discussion?
Consistent membership to allow the group to mature?
Only those with expertise in this area?
....
....

3 What is the brief or terms of reference of the meeting?
Does this meeting have the power to take a decision?
Can this meeting make a recommendation?
How wide can the discussion usefully range?
Is there a decision relating to this topic already made that cannot be changed?
Are there some conclusions that would be unacceptable? To whom?
....
....

4 What is the agenda for this meeting?
What do we need to consider?
Is there too much here?
Who has access to putting items on the agenda?
Which order should things come in?
Who gets a copy?

Will matters arising and any other business take up a lot of time?

....

....

5 What about the physical location and arrangements?
Have we identified a room and does everyone know which?
Can everyone see everyone else and give/receive eye contact?
Is there something to write on?
Is it noisy/hot/cold/likely to have interruptions?
Can everyone get there in the time allowed?

....

....

6 Who makes a contribution?
Who has something to say?
How can I keep the long-winded brief?
How can I get the time to contribute?
When should I nudge the meeting towards a decision/the next item?
How will individuals indicate they want a turn?

....

....

7 Minutes or report of the meeting
Who writes these?
Should they just list actions decided and the name of person responsible?
Is it important to describe the discussion and issues?
Who gets a copy?
Do people other than participants or regular circulation receive a copy if they are affected by an issue discussed (eg Caretaker)?
What will be the effect of these minutes on those people who attended/did not attend?
Who are we trying to influence with these minutes?

....

....

8 Implementation of proposals

Who has agreed to do what?
How can we help each other to get on with it?
Who else can we involve?
How can we monitor the implementation?
Doe we need a review date?
What can I do to get things moving?

....

....

9 Calendar for future meetings

How often do we need to meet?
Could sub-groups meet?
What other meetings do the members have to attend?
Do we want a regular time or do we wait until we have an agenda?
Is our cycle of need different from the norm?

....

....

10 And finally . . .

Is the meeting really necessary or could we use our time better?
Is a meeting the best way of achieving the declared objectives?

....

....

9 Job definition and individual feedback: how teachers know what their job is

The increasing speed of change in schools means that most teachers find their jobs changing around them. They frequently lose certainty about what they should be doing, why and how. The approach of this exercise is to take a group of between five and 15, discuss the general problem of job clarity and then develop understanding of methods to deal with the problem by discussing four different situations. The group brainstorms to identify a range of methods of approach and finally each member of the group produces their own list of three methods they will use in the next term.

On completion of this exercise participants should be able to:

a) identify various methods for preventing individuals being unsure of what their priorities should be;
b) decide three methods to use in the next term.

Participants will need:
Job Document I – *Particular individuals*
Goal Planning Sheets (see page 7)

To the trainer

Recent changes in schools have meant that many teachers have diversified from teaching just their own subject. With falling rolls there is an increasing need for teachers to teach a second and third subject – with the attendant extra work of belonging to several departments. The rise of PSE has involved many teachers in this new area. Special Needs and Section 11 provisions have meant some teachers working with particular pupils rather than particular subjects. How do teachers know which of this plethora of jobs is theirs?

Introduction

Invite groups to discuss the following points (20 minutes):

1 One of the main tensions in teaching is between the claim to be professional (with the concomitant attributes of being able to decide what, when, how and where this professionalism is practised) and the obvious fact of a hierarchy as laid down by job titles and salary scales. This second implies that those towards the top have some organisational or managerial responsibility which, in turn, suggests that they have some control over what people do. The two attributes are mutually incompatible in their absolute forms and an uneasy compromise exists in most schools. The 1987 anguish over teacher contracts perhaps demonstrates the depth of emotions involved.

2 Teachers are doing a *large number of jobs* as well as that of teaching particular subjects to a group of pupils. Some we found were:
   - Administration of tutor groups
   - Development of teaching materials
   - Paper work
   - Organisation of one-off events
   - Support for other members of staff
   - Contact with other agencies

3 Individual teachers *acquire* jobs to do and are informed of this in various formal and informal ways, for example:
   - Staff handbook
   - Statutory requirements
   - Department/Year meetings
   - Request from senior staff or head of department
   - Timetable
   - Voluntary involvement
   - Jobs inherited from previous job holder

Symptoms of problem

With this plethora of possible jobs to do, coupled with the professional/ managed conundrum, is it any wonder that some teachers get over-loaded and feel overworked? In some teachers this can lead to the symptoms of stress: illness and absenteeism. Other teachers feel bewildered that their efforts have not been recognised by the obvious signs of time, money, resources or thanks – nor have they effected change. All of this, in some cases, leads to embittered staff who become destructive and 'switched off'. Others feel they are running around getting nowhere. This may be because they have a mismatched jumble of jobs that it does not make sense for one person to be doing. How can these teachers make sense of it all and ask for help?

Document I: Particular individuals

Hand out copies of Document I and generate discussion about each of the individuals in turn (15 to 20 minutes each).

Particular issues to draw out about each are:

1 Helen – Besides the national and individual factors mentioned previously, Helen has gone from a low timetable and lots of systematic support in her probationary year to a full timetable and no systematic support. She is left alone to sort out the demands and requests on her time and skills. She has become overloaded and now feels a failure. Yet her only failure was in appearing so confident, competent and keen that more and more was expected of her. No-one helped her make sense of this.
2 Gary – If someone had either used Gary's skills to aid the introduction of computing in administration or explained why he was not being included, perhaps his energies would still be organisationally functional whereas they are in danger of becoming dysfunctional.
3 Doreen – Doreen's teaching role requires her to give consistent, continuous attention to the 30 or so pupils in her classroom. This role has become particularly demanding with the newer methodologies of investigative and discussion-type teaching. Yet her constant interruptions can only be coped with in the more traditional, formal styles of teaching that are considered old-fashioned and out of date in this school. No-one is helping Doreen make sense of her two incompatible roles.
4 Peter and John – Talking to them and observing them it is clear that Peter and John are quite unsure what their role in a participative decision-making system should be: brake, resourcer, instigator, personnel manager, broker, administrator, disciplinarian. They have no-one with whom to discuss this.

Preparing an action list

1 Ask groups to brainstorm different methods that could be used for letting individuals know what are the important things they need to do at work. (See Introduction on how to run brainstorming.)

Examples are:
• Job descriptions
• Performance appraisal
• A Deputy Headteacher who looks out for younger staff to warn them of getting overloaded ie making it legitimate to say no.

- An annual personal review with Head of Department/Head of Year and Senior Staff – not just about careers.
- A half-termly meeting of Head of Department, Headteacher and Deputy Headteacher, enabling a review of what is going on and providing a chance to discuss and decide the priority of jobs.
- Informal talks in the staffroom between personal contacts. In one school a Head of Special Needs filled this role for a lot of people within the school.

2 Give out copies of the goal planning sheet. Ask each member of the group to identify three of the suggested methods that they will try to use in the next term. (This should take about 10 minutes per person.)

The important thing is to discuss not only *what*, but *how* they are going to implement this. This may well include training in specific techniques. You could use the goal planning exercise given in the Introduction to do this.

Some jobs are taken on voluntarily and others through direction. The difficulty is to ensure that:

- all necessary jobs are done;
- not too many unnecessary jobs are done;
- the total package of jobs being done by one person makes sense.

It is this third point which is the concern of this exercise.

Job definition Document I: Particular individuals

Examples of particular individuals at different stages in their careers in different schools. (We include four examples to demonstrate that the issue occurs at all levels in the hierarchy. Of course you may decide just to use two of them.)

1 **Helen**
Last year, after completing her probationary year on a low timetable, Helen volunteered for all sorts of extra tasks, including organising a 'day' for the whole school on Nicaragua. She was an active member of the school band and plays and was always ready to see pupils at lunch time and after school. She had volunteered for some of the more difficult fourth and fifth year groups. We met her in her seventh term of teaching. She was having problems with a fourth year group and a Deputy Head has taken over. She is now off work sick about 40% of the time. She complains of being tired and is seriously thinking of leaving the profession.

Points for discussion:
- Why has a keen, lively, energetic teacher become tired and disillusioned so quickly?
- Is there anything the particular school could have done to help?
- How would you help Helen?

2 **Gary**
Gary is in his late twenties, teaching Maths and Computing. His enthusiasm for computing has led him to develop all sorts of systems for whole-school use, eg lists of children, timetabling, exam options. He has a knack of seeing where computing could relieve teachers of day-to-day administrative tasks. A computing system was introduced into the administration office by the LEA and the Head and he was not involved at all. Gary cannot understand why, with his experience and expertise, he was not consulted. He has started putting satiric writing on the staff notice board and is becoming embittered.

Point for discussion:
- What would you do to keep Gary involved in the school?

3 **Doreen**
Doreen is joint Head of House and teaches an 80% timetable. Her lessons are constantly interrupted by the 'phone in her

© Derek Torrington, Jane Weightman, Basil Blackwell Ltd, 1989.

room or people coming in with messages about pupils in her House. She feels she is doing neither job properly and that somehow she is to blame for not being better organised. She looks very harassed and worn.*

Point for discussion:
● How can Doreen's work be sorted out?

4 Peter and John

Peter and John are Deputy Headteachers in a school which has a participative system of decision-making. All staff are entitled to attend all meetings and have the power to make policy. For example, the decision on how to select for a particular promotion was decided by a meeting and the selectors appointed by this meeting — it included John and five other teachers. Peter and John teach a 50% timetable compared to the school norm of 85%. The school has good non-teaching assistance. Both Peter and John come to school at 7.30 am and leave at 6ish. They both talked about how very busy and stressed they are but were the most nervous of all our observees about being interviewed and observed.

Points for discussion:
● What should their role be?
● Who should help them decide this?

* It seems an inevitable part of the role of Head of Year/House that they pick up on the day-to-day variations, uncertainties and hiccups in schools. Every school we visited was trying to devolve this back to form tutors but we would suggest that as we found this problem so universal it may be that by having the role of Head of Year/Head of House the problem is created. They become the receivers of the school's irritants and these can only be dealt with successfully that day, not delayed.

Goal Planning Sheet

GOAL. . . . .

STRENGTHS	NEEDS

NEED. . . . .

OBJECTIVE	METHOD OF TACKLING	TARGET DATE	DATE DONE

10 Appraisal: how teachers know how they are doing

This set of materials is more varied than most in the book and has a greater degree of structure. It constitutes an introductory training course for all those involved in teacher appraisal and would be best used over a full day or two half days. Because of the hopes and fears surrounding the topic, there needs to be a thorough introduction and we offer two alternative introductory talks. Trainers will make their own judgements about how much of each to use. There are then three sequential exercises in developing interview practice for both appraisers and appraisees. All the materials are non-threatening and we would not advocate using closed-circuit television.

On completion participants will be able to:

a) understand different approaches to the appraisal process;
b) appreciate the objectives and some of the problems of appraisal;
c) understand how the appraisal interview can be used to elicit information and provide feedback;
d) participate in an appraisal interview as appraiser or appraisee;
e) identify and practise specific aspects of interview skill.

Participants will need:
Appraisal Document I – *Basic appraisal skills*
Appraisal Document II – *Demands, choices and constraints*
Appraisal Document III – *Constructs activity*
Appraisal Document IV – *Mini-appraisal interview*

To the trainer

The material in this unit is designed for use in introducing staff to the appraisal process, hence there is quite a lot of diverse material, including notes for introductory talks by the trainer. The subject of appraisal needs both explanation and discussion to overcome the deep reservations held by many and the genuine anxieties of a few. It also needs practice in *appraisal* interviewing and being interviewed in *an appraisal context*.

The materials for interview practice are usable by any group of people, but trainers may well wish to use other, local materials that will be appropriate in their particular situation. This set of materials probably needs more personal shaping by the trainer than those in other units in this book.

First of all there are notes for two different introductory talks by the trainer, with suggestions for discussion.

Introduction

Begin by introducing the subject, using one of the 'trainer talks' outlined below, or a combination.

Trainer Talk I: Problems and opportunities in appraisal

Teachers are very diligent in giving pupils feedback about their performance: marking books, commenting on performance during class, keeping records and writing reports home about the individual child. It is surprising, then, that virtually no systematic feedback is given to teachers about their own performance once they have passed through the probationary period. This is partly due to the idea of the independent professional who needs no appraisal and partly to the difficulty of finding a suitable way of appraising performance, not least because appraisal involves both *judgement* and *reporting*; neither of which is invariably reliable.

Reasons why seniors may wish to appraise juniors in an organisation are:

- *Human resources considerations* – to ensure that the abilities and energies of individuals are being effectively used
- *Training* – identifying training needs so the contribution of individuals may be developed
- *Promotion* – appraisal can assist decision making
- *Planning* – to identify skill shortages and succession needs.
- *Authority* – appraisal sustains the hierarchy of authority by confirming the dependence of subordinates on those who carry out the appraisals

Are there any other reasons we can add to that list?

Reasons why juniors may wish to be appraised by their seniors in an organisation are:

- *Performance* – ability to do the job may be enhanced by an emphasis on strengths and an understanding of what changes are needed.

- *Motivation* – reassurance can increase the level of enthusiasm and commitment to the job.
- *Career* – individuals can get guidance and indicators about possible job changes.

Are there any other reasons we can add to that list?

There are, however, problems associated with appraisal systems. For those carrying out the appraisal, many things can impair their judgement or reporting. For example: prejudice; insufficient knowledge of the appraisee; the 'halo effect' of general likeability or recent events; the difficulty of distinguishing appraisees from the context in which they work; different perceptions of which standards are appropriate.

Problems for both the appraiser and the appraisee include: the amount of paperwork associated with any scheme aiming at reporting consistently; and the formality which the interview requires, to distinguish it from the informal chat in the corridor.

Experience in other organisations has shown that appraisal schemes fail because: outcomes are ignored; everyone is 'just above average'; there is incomplete coverage of the constituency; or behaviours other than the real work are evaluated (such as time-keeping, looking busy and being pleasant) because they are easier to see.

Despite these problems, the potential advantages of performance appraisal are so great that attempts are continually being made to make it work. The problem-solving approach, discussed on page 93, is the most effective, providing that both the appraiser and appraisee have the skill and ability to handle this mode. This approach is similar to counselling as neither of the parties knows 'the answer' before the interview begins: it develops by the process of interaction itself.

Trainer Talk II: Contrasted views of appraisal

There are two contrasted views of appraisal: the *control* and the *personal*. The control is the most common, but the personal is rapidly gaining popularity. Increasingly, appraisal schemes have elements of both approaches, but describing them as polar opposites helps to illustrate the key elements.

1 The *control approach* starts with an expression of opinion by someone 'up there', who represents the view of controlling, responsible authority: 'We must stimulate effective performance and develop potential, set targets to be achieved, reward above-average achievement and ensure that promotion is based on sound criteria.'

   That type of initiative is almost always resisted by people acting collectively, despite its specious appeal. This is because people construe the message in a way that is seldom intended by the controlling authorities, like this: 'They will put pressure on poor performers so that they improve or leave. They will also make sure that people do what they're told. We will all be vulnerable to individual managerial whim and prejudice, losing a bit more control over our individual destiny.'

This approach is likely to engender:

a) conflictual behaviour and attitudes;
b) negotiated modifications to schemes, frequently making them ineffective;
c) tight bureaucratic controls to ensure consistency and fairness of reported judgements;
d) bland, safe statements in the appraisal process;
e) little impact on actual performance, except on that of a minority of self-assured high achievers at one extreme and disenchanted idlers at the other. Otherwise it tends to encourage people to play safe and go by the book;
f) reduced trust, loyalty and initiative.

This approach works best when there are clear and specific targets for people to reach, within an organisational culture that emphasises competition. There are considerable problems, for example: Who sets the standards and who makes the judgements? How are the judgements, by different appraisers of different appraisees, made consistent? Despite its drawbacks, this approach is still potentially useful as a system of keeping records and providing a framework for career development that is an improvement on references and panel interviews. It works best in bureaucracies.

The emphasis is on *form-filling*.

2 The *personal approach* starts with a question in the mind of the individual job holder: 'I am not sure whether I am doing a good job or not. I would like to find ways of doing the job better, if I can, and I would like to clarify and improve my career prospects.'

But this question is addressed by job holders *to themselves*. Not: 'Please sir, what did I get for my French homework?', but, 'Where can I find someone to talk through with me my plans, my progress, my hopes, my fears? Who can help me come to terms with my limitations and understand my mistakes? Where can I find someone with the experience and wisdom to discuss my performance with me so that I can shape it, building on my strengths to improve the fit between what I can contribute and what the organisation needs from me?'

This approach works best with people who are professionally

competent and self-assured, so that they can generate constructive criticism in discussion with a peer; or in protégé/mentor situations, where there is high mutual respect.

Some, however, are suspicious of this approach, feeling that 'This leads to people doing what they want to do rather than what they should be doing. There is no co-ordination, no comparison and no satisfactory management control.'

This approach to appraisal:

a) develops co-operative behaviour and autonomous responsibility;
b) confronts issues, seeking to resolve problems;
c) does not work well with bureaucratic control;
d) produces searching analysis;
e) impacts directly and constructively on performance;
f) requires high trust, engenders loyalty and stimulates initiative.

The benefits of this type of appraisal can be enormous but there are two problems: first, lack of systematic reporting; second, where are the paragons in whom you can trust?

The emphasis is on *interviewing*.

Points for discussion:
● *To what extent can the benefits of both approaches be created in a single scheme?*
● *Who should conduct the appraisal interview?*

Basic interview skills

The objective of this exercise is for people to practise the basic skills of the appraisal interview. You can run the exercise either in pairs or in small groups of three with one person acting as observer. With experienced staff you might ask them to select two of the exercises to try. The emphasis is on the basic techniques of interviewing, to act as a reminder or refresher for staff. This takes about an hour for two exercises.

1 Give each person a copy of Document I and ask them to spend some time reading through the interview skills.
2 Hand out Document II and ask pairs/trios to conduct interviews as outlined on the sheet.
3 Ask pairs/trios to discuss what they have done.
   (20 minutes)

Points for discussion:
● At what *stages* in the appraisal interview would you be likely to use closed questions and probes?

- For what *topics* in the interview would you use open-ended questions, direct questions and probes?
  (20 minutes)

Content of the interview

Give each person a copy of Documents III and IV. The aim here is for participants to talk about their own jobs. These exercises are techniques for doing so.

Staff should work in pairs to experiment with the two techniques, with A using Document III to interview B and B using Document IV to interview A. This will take one and a half hours.

The mini appraisal interview

Give each person a copy of Document V. Again, group people to work in pairs, or possibly threes. The document focuses on the first week of term, but ideally the topic should be suited to the particular situation of the participants. Alternatives might be: liaison with other schools; new staff; induction of new pupils . . . This takes at least two hours.

Conclusion

A final discussion among all participants could focus on the various issues that have been developed during the course, including one from the last exercise:

- How useful did you find it to discuss an aspect of your work with someone who was well-informed, but not your 'boss'? Would it have been more or less useful to have that discussion with your boss?

Appraisal Document I – Basic appraisal skills

Some of the methods to be used in appraisal interviewing are found in other types of interviewing as well. The following are especially important.

Rapport

The appraiser establishes an atmosphere in which effective interaction can take place between the appraiser and appraisee.

The prospect of the interview is likely to make the appraisee apprehensive, both because it may be necessary to face up to difficult questions, and because the outcomes could be personally significant. The appraiser should therefore spend a short time setting up the interview with preliminary exchanges that will make the process more constructive. Typical methods are:

a) Friendly, easy manner
b) Attentiveness
c) Small talk
d) Calmness
e) Smile and eye contact
f) Explaining procedure

Appraisers should avoid being patronising ('Now there's nothing to worry about...') or emphasising their own superiority ('You don't need to be afraid of *me*.'). This type of comment is likely to be interpreted as indicating that there IS something to worry about.

Listening

As well as hearing what is said, the appraiser listens to pick up on aspects that are not clear, to select matters which need to be followed up and constantly to focus the appraisee's thinking and articulation.

Typical methods are:

a) Interest
b) Eye behaviour (opening wide, narrowing, eyebrows raised or furrowed etc) and encouraging noises ('Ummm', 'Ah', 'Yes', 'I see'...) to develop a particular line of comment.
c) Keeping silent except for providing focus to the appraisee.

Closed questions

The appraiser asks closed questions to obtain information. Closed questions are those seeking precise facts, and which deny the opportunity to elaborate.
Examples:

a) 'How many are doing GCSE Chemistry this year?'
b) 'When do you start your new job?'
c) 'Where did you train?'

Open-ended questions

The appraiser asks open-ended questions in order to invite the appraisee to open up on a topic.
Open-ended questions are the most fruitful for appraisers to develop an understanding of the appraisee, who is encouraged to tell the story in his or her own way, with personal selection of what to include, what to emphasise and what to omit.
Examples:

a) 'What is happening with the current project?'
b) 'What is involved in your present post?'
c) 'How do you run the . . .?'

Follow-up questions

The appraiser asks follow-up questions to develop and focus the answer to an open-ended question.
The appraiser needs to ask follow-up questions either to encourage the diffident to say more or to pin down a point on which the appraisee appears uneasy.
Typical methods are:

a) Reminder follow-up ('And what about . . .?')
b) Forced-choice follow-up ('So where does your main interest lie, in the 'A' level work or GCSE?')
c) Second step follow-up ('So what was the main benefit to you in producing the school play?')

Direct questions

The appraiser asks direct questions demanding both a reply and precision.
Sometimes it is necessary to push an appraisee to confront an issue that is being avoided, for instance:

a) 'Why did you leave that job?'
b) 'When will you let me know?'
c) 'Did you or didn't you?'

Summary and re-run
The appraiser draws together in summary various of the appraisee's points and obtains confirmation of the appraiser's understanding.

This device enables the appraiser to check understanding by picking out what appear to be the main points mentioned in the immediate past stage of the interview, summarising them, and asking for confirmation that they have been correctly understood. This also demonstrates attention and accurate listening. It provides a good opportunity to move the interview on to a different topic area, for instance:

a) 'So the new Head of Department did not see eye to eye with you and you felt the time had come for a move; but in retrospect you are not so sure?'
b) 'So you think the problem with the fifth years has been the change of exam board rather than the changes of staff?'

Probes

The appraiser questions to obtain information the respondent would prefer to conceal.

Those with skeletons in the cupboard (especially imaginary ones) become adept at deflecting questions intended to bring the skeletons out! The appraiser then has to consider the question 'Do I persist?'. Is it reasonable to press the appraisee to respond to a question, or should the desire for privacy be respected? If it is decided to continue, the following methods are recommended:

a) Direct questions, as described above.
b) Supplementary questions where even a direct question has been deflected.
c) Face-saving close when the reply has eventually come.

A thoroughly disreputable practice, very rarely used as an alternative to the above, is to over-state the assumption, like this:

Question: 'There appears to be a gap in your record at the end of 1985. You weren't in prison or anything were you?'
Answer: 'Good Heavens, no. I was having treatment for . . . er . . . well, alcoholism actually.'

© Derek Torrington, Jane Weightman, Basil Blackwell Ltd, 1989.

The undesirable is rapidly substituted for the unacceptable. It is a very effective technique, but never found in the teaching profession (well, hardly ever . . .).

Braking

The appraiser uses 'braking' to slow the rate of response from the respondent.

Rapport, careful listening and open-ended questions encourage people to talk. Few teachers need any encouragement to talk anyway, so appraisers can find the appraisal going on and on. How do you apply the brakes without 'losing' the appraisee through suddenly appearing abrupt and authoritarian? The following is a hierarchy of techniques that get gradually more drastic:

a) Ask closed questions that simply break the rhythm
b) Adopt the furrowed brow of (slight) professional anxiety
c) Stare in glazed abstraction (as demonstrated by any third year on Friday afternoons)
d) Look away, or glance at your watch
e) Interrupt the speaker

Appraisal Document II – Practice in basic skills

Document I lists the basic skills of the appraisal interview. The purpose of this exercise is to practise those skills. In a pair, take it in turns to play the leading role. In a trio, take turns in the leading role, respondent role and observer role.

1 Listening/summary and re-run

Preparation
A and B both prepare a brief statement (one minute) on a controversial issue outside education.

Activity
A makes his/her statement.
B re-states it, reflecting A's views as accurately as possible.
A corrects B as necessary until A is satisfied that B understands what A's point of view is and has summarised it accurately.

Repeat, with B making the opening statement.

2 Asking open-ended questions/follow-up questions

Preparation
The aim is to ask questions that will keep someone talking purposefully and informatively for five minutes. Prepare one or two open-ended questions on how something is done in your partner's school – curriculum, organisation, etc.

Activity
A puts open-ended question to B and develops answer with follow-up questions.
After five minutes the observer comments on the amount of focus and development that was offered, how it was used and the general effectiveness of the exchange.
Repeat, with B asking A.

3 Asking direct questions/probing

Preparation
The aim is to find out about your partner's views on an issue in education. Partners may agree on the topic beforehand. Ideally it should be a controversial issue. Prepare appropriate questions (three minutes).

© Derek Torrington, Jane Weightman, Basil Blackwell Ltd, 1989.

Activity

A puts a direct question (or questions) to B and follows up with probes to get a clear understanding of B's views. The questioning should be completed with a summary and re-run.
Repeat, with B asking A.

4 Asking closed questions

Preparation

The aim is to find out as much as possible in one minute about your partner's work in school. Work on a series of questions to elicit this information (three minutes).

Activity

A puts questions to B.
Repeat, with B asking A.
Observer initiates discussion on the relative effectiveness of each enquiry by comparing the amount of information disclosed.

Appraisal Document III: Demands, constraints and choices

Demands

What are the demands of your job? That is, the things that *have* to be done by you. They cannot be ignored, delegated or passed on. What are the penalties for not doing them? It might help to think of the following areas:

1 People working with you
2 Senior staff
3 Peers
4 People outside the school
5 Administration – procedures and meetings
6 Others

Constraints

What are the constraints that stop you developing your job in absolutely the way you would like? For example:

1 The resources, such as buildings
2 Legal restrictions
3 Technical limitations of equipment
4 Physical location
5 School/LEA policies and procedures
6 Attitude of others
7 Other

Choices

What are the choices available to you about *what* you do, *how* you do it and *when* you do it?

1 Within your department
2 With your peers
3 To protect the unit from disturbance
4 Upwards
5 Elsewhere in the school
6 Outside the school
7 Other

Based on R Stewart, *Choices for Managers*, McGraw Hill, 1981.

Appraisal Document IV: Constructs activity

1 Preparation by A:
Write down the response to the following questions on separate cards or pieces of paper:

a) Name an activity you perform in your job that is very important (this should be a verb, not a role or responsibility).
b) Name an activity you do frequently – not necessarily important, but which occupies a good deal of time.
c) Name an activity, though important, unlikely to appear in your diary.
d) What is the most important activity not listed so far?

2 Interview/discussion led by B on the following topics:

- How are a and b similar and how are they different?
- What makes them easier, or harder, to do than c?
- Which is it more important in your job to do well: b or c?
- On what criteria did you select d?
- Which gives you most satisfaction, a, b, c or d?

Based on A and V Stewart, *Tomorrow's Managers Today*, IPM, 1981.

Appraisal Document V: A mini appraisal interview

The subject for this interview is the first week of this term. You may look at all the work of the first week or some part of it.

1 A interviews B for information about their first week. (15 minutes)
2 B interviews A for information about their first week. (15 minutes)
3 A and B prepare for feedback and discussion. (15 minutes)
4 B conducts appraisal interview with A about the first week of term. (30 minutes +)
5 A conducts appraisal interview with B about the first week of term. (30 minutes +)
6 A and B discuss what they liked and disliked about the process.

Points to remember:
The first interview is for information gathering – you might use some of the ideas explored in previous sessions.

The second interview is for feedback. This should include looking for good practice. Only criticise those things that can be changed.

11 Communications I: purposes and methods

This set of materials is for a thorough and systematic examination of how communication works in the school, using a well-tried method of analysis and offering detailed examples. It is suggested for a group ranging in size from five to 30, but it is also a useful and viable exercise for an individual.

On completion participants should be able to:

a) distinguish between different reasons for communication;
b) determine modes of communication to suit different purposes and groups.

Participants will need:
Communications/purpose Document I – *Examples of schools*
Communications/purpose Document II – *Blank grid*
Communications/purpose Document III – *Examples of bulletins*

To the trainer

Consider these typical snatches of everyday school conversation:

'Nobody ever tells me anything . . .!'
'The kids always seem to know before us . . .'
'On no, not more bumph in my pigeonhole . . .'
'. . . I'm sorry, I didn't know about it . . .' 'Well, you really should have; it was in last week's bulletin.'

These remarks exemplify the problems of communication in any large and complex organisation such as a comprehensive school. On a human-relations measure it seems impossible to satisfy everyone all the time, and on an efficiency measure it seems equally impossible to ensure that the message always gets through. This can be very annoying and perplexing to the few individuals who can justifiably pride themselves on their efficiency in this respect. No matter how well-designed the system of communication looks on paper, there will always be occasions when it breaks down. We should not be too surprised about this, as people are only human after all, but there is usually some way of improving an organisation's communications, even if perfection is unattainable.

The purpose of communication is not only to keep people informed; it is also the main means of influencing each other's behaviour. Communication is therefore an important part of the management and organisation of schools as we try to influence each other to agreed action.

The question 'How do you find out what's going on?' provokes various replies:

Bill and Ben

Often the reply to this question is something like: 'Oh, I generally ask Bill, or Ben; they usually seem to know what's going on'. Here we have the growth of an informal network of 'ears and mouthpieces' of management, or the *Bill and Ben system.*

Noisy plumbing

In other cases the answer is something like: 'Oh, my Head of Department sometimes tells me if he thinks it's something I need to know. Isn't that the way it's supposed to work?'

Indeed it is, but it does not work very reliably. With these bureaucratic 'cascade' systems, much depends on the people controlling the 'taps' at each level. All too often the staff on the ground floor are without water, or else it arrives over-filtered or even polluted.

Just a minute!

One method of finding out what is going on is through the minutes of meetings. Traditionally, minutes are issued only to those who attended the meeting or sent apologies for absence. But another view is to regard minutes as a means of communication, as well as a record. Several schools are experimenting with supplying copies of minutes of all meetings to all staff. Those that are interested will read them; others will throw them away.

The legibility test

In one school, we saw examples of minutes hastily written up by a deputy in untidy long-hand just before the next meeting ('I've been too busy'). The document looked like some weird psychological test. It was then photocopied for distribution at the meeting. Not surprisingly, the meeting got off to a rather spotty start.

Introduction

Generate discussion in your group for about 15 minutes, using some of the above examples to get things going.

Points for discussion:
- In the last week have there been examples of frustrated communication?
- Why was this?
- How could this have been improved?

Now move on to talk about the *purposes* of meetings.

Media for communication – Examples of schools

1 Introduce the exercise by explaining that Greenbaum (1974) suggests that managers have four main objectives for organisational communication. These can be applied to school situations as follows:

Regulation – seeking conformity to school rules and objectives
Innovation – seeking to change aspects of the school in particular ways
Integration – maintaining morale, culture and ethos
Information – passing on mainly factual information needed to do the work

2 Give members of the group Document I.
3 Ask groups to work through the various sections to clarify that everyone understands the meaning of regulation/innovation/ integration and information. (10–15 minutes)

Discussion points
- Compare the use of non-verbal communication at the two schools. What does this say about the sorts of culture that exist?
- Is there any difference between the schools in their regulation communication?
- How does this compare with the examples given about integration?

Purpose of communication: Documents II and III

The main purpose of this exercise is for the group to analyse some real examples of communication in schools. This can be done with a tape-recording of a staff briefing, a video of some interaction in school, or role play. Examples of schools with *written* communication are provided in Document III.

1 Give out copies of Document III and invite staff participants to discuss the examples:

Westcliffe has a particularly good staff bulletin. It is a major device for communicating across the school. It is published every Thursday lunchtime (after the Wednesday afternoon Senior Management Committee (SMG) meeting). Items have to be with the respective Deputy Head the day before; anyone can put anything in. It includes factual information about children leaving, trips, appointments, articles from various members of staff seeking assistance with resources and items for sale. It also includes points for discussion, such as minutes of meetings or ideas for reorganisation from individuals or groups of staff. The bulletin is used and read by staff. The SMG reserve the right to reply in the bulletin but all items are published.

Hall End has daily bulletins distributed to each member of staff through the pigeonholes. Anyone can enter items and they have to be with the Deputy Head the previous lunchtime.

2 Give out Document II and get the group to fill in the appropriate part of the grid for the examples given. (Obviously this will be 'whole organisation – written' for the bulletins.) Ask groups to go through each item of the example and see which sort of communication it is. (30 minutes)
3 Initiate a general discussion comparing the two examples. For example,

Westcliffe has a wider distribution of contributors; it also has integration.

Hall End is mostly information/regulation.

Encourage members to think of other ways in which the same purposes might have been effectively served.

Blank grid – own school

Give each member a second copy of the blank grid and ask them to collect examples from their school or department. This can either be done within the session or taken away and brought back on another occasion for discussion. If done within the session allow about 45 minutes to fill in the grids. We suggest small groups of four or five to do this. Encourage them to think of examples for each of the squares.

Points for discussion
- Which medium is most effective for which purpose and for which size of group?
- For which purpose is it most difficult to think of examples?
- For which medium is it most difficult to think of examples?
- For which grouping is it most difficult to think of examples?
- What does this tell you about your school?

Conclusion

1 Ask each member which area of communication they are going to think about more in the next week.
2 Summarise the purpose of the activity: by considering how people in schools communicate about regulation, innovation, integration and information to individuals, groups and the whole school, one learns a lot about how people in that school handle the central issues. For example, the quantity and quality of communication on regulations will show where they are on the control/autonomy dimension. What is communicated about integration will show the nature of the culture, co-ordination, cohesiveness and valuing in the school. Similarly, the kind of communication about innovation can tell us something about participation and change and we can ask whether information about resources is exchanged. So this communications grid can help to examine a school's approach to the wider issues of management and organisation. Conversely, this grid forms a helpful planning device, prompting us to think about each of the squares and whether some appropriate method is used or should be initiated.

References

Greenbaum, HW (1974), 'The Audit of Organisational Communication', *Academy of Management Journal*, pp. 739–54.

Communications/purpose Document I: Examples of schools

Oakhill school

		Regulation	Innovation	Integration	Information
Face to face (2)	ORAL	One supply to another on grade slips for 2/3 yr	DHT to HT re 3rd Yr gps	DHT saying hello to stranger in staffroom	Staff phoning when absent
	WRITTEN	Timetable cover list			Details about detentions in book of register each am for tutor
	NON-VERBAL	Lights outside HT office	Change of name to Br Bilal by Rastafarian teacher	DHT to Prob. after inspectors being there and smiling	

		Regulation	Innovation	Integration	Information
Small groups (3–10)	ORAL	H of English keeping people to agenda	Hum. Meeting new books change exam paper	Eng. Dept. meet new HoD at old HoD house	Dept. meetings. Talk of children in staffroom
	WRITTEN	3rd Yr × curriculum Eng. project syllabus – all had contributed	Profile records from another school to 5th Yr tutors		Agenda circulated to Eng. Dept. before meeting
	NON-VERBAL		Spec. Needs had no room, to show new role ie support not withdrawal	Integ. Curric. prep. room being sorted out so easier to use	Grouping subjects together in corridors

		Regulation	Innovation	Integration	Information
Whole organisation	ORAL	Morning briefing: do not lock rooms on yale key	INSET plenary times of day	Staff meeting Pl after half term	Morning briefing: children suspended
	WRITTEN	School bulletin. Register of staff in staffroom	INSET documents asking for replies	Noticeboard for political, social, action non-school activities	School bulletin – weekly events, eg visits
	NON-VERBAL	HT not available to staff without appointment or outside school hours		Having a pass key – but some doors on special keys!	Lack of numbers on map led to lost supply teachers

2 Summerfield High

		Regulation	Innovation	Integration	Information
	ORAL	HT and H PE re PTR – HT tells him he is best but for craft	H of SN to H Eng. about materials for remedial children	DHT seeing all supply teachers first thing	HoD telling supply where worksheets are
Face to face (2)	WRITTEN	Note from HT asking A to come to see him	H of SN giving materials for H Eng. to try out		List of materials needed for lessons given to technician
	NON-VERBAL	Display in DSN to suggest diff. ways of working with these children	Doors open between labs so can chat, pop in out, jokes		Pointing to where classroom is

		Regulation	Innovation	Integration	Information
	ORAL		HT to Hum. Dept. about new options leads Integ. Hum.	H. Eng. inviting dept. to her house for party	HoD to Dept. about GCSE course
Small groups (3–10)	WRITTEN	Marking scheme in Eng. Dept.	H of ML passing round letters he received re courses etc in ML meeting		Dept. Handbook Eng. Dept.
	NON-VERBAL			Arrangement of chairs in Pastoral Room and its existence ie 1 not 5	

		Regulation	Innovation	Integration	Information
	ORAL	Finance – DHT asks for weighting, HT says we'll talk about it individ. ie no	Curric. Planning meeting Role of DSN – leads to working party	Jokes before school eg photo on ski trip	Weekly briefing
Whole organ-isation	WRITTEN	Cover list with daily notes eg change of assembly because gym new floor	Agenda for curric. planning in bulletin 2 weeks before therefore consult	Parody of bulletin although misfire with SMG – become 'fable' status	Bulletin weekly
	NON-VERBAL		Gym new floor meant rearrange rooms	Photos of ski trip Use of Lib. for staff briefing	

Purpose of communication – Document II: Blank grid

		Regulation	Innovation	Integration	Information
Face to face (2)	**ORAL**				
	WRITTEN				
	NON-VERBAL				
Small groups (3–10)	**ORAL**				
	WRITTEN				
	NON-VERBAL				
Whole organisation	**ORAL**				
	WRITTEN				
	NON-VERBAL				

Purpose of communication – Document III: Examples of bulletins

```
WESTCLIFFE SCHOOL

THE BULLETIN

No. 36 1985/86

25th June, 1986
```

1   DIARY

Monday, 30th June   Diary or Progress File Check for Upper School
                       Tutor Groups Joint 1st/2nd Year Assembly

Tuesday, 1st July   6th year Assembly – Lecture Theatre
                       Progress File check for Lower School Tutor Groups

Wednesday, 2nd July   3rd Year Assembly – Gym
                       2nd Year Assembly
                       SMG Meeting Upper School, 4.00 p.m.

Thursday, 3rd July

Friday, 4th July   4th Year Assembly – Gym
                       1st Year Assembly

2   COPYRIGHT LOGBOOKS – FROM PHIL ABRAHAM (DHT)

Whilst colleagues are now getting into the habit of entering copyright Xeroxing into the Logbook in Upper School, there is a marked absence of entries in the Lower School Logbook. The same restrictions apply (copies of the Licence are alongside both machines), and colleagues in Lower School should make sure that all relevant work is entered.

3   FIRE DRILL – FROM MARGARET BATTERSBY (ST)

A timetable and lists of Upper School classes taking place in Lower School are now housed in both Upper and Lower School offices, and will be available with the registers in the event of a fire alarm.

4   FROM JILL CORN (HOY 5) – YOUTHSCAN UK

If you are observant you will have noticed the name *Youthscan* on the substitution list this week.

© Derek Torrington, Jane Weightman, Basil Blackwell Ltd, 1989.

It is a national study of all children born 5th–11th April 1970, originating from the 1970 Birth Chart of the National Birthday Trust Fund. It investigates such issues as education, transition from school to employment, health, food and diet, spare-time activities, money, smoking, etc.

Three 5th Year students are doing tests and questionnaires, etc., this week in connection with this and are also being interviewed at home with their parents by the school nurse.

5   ARCHAEOLOGY EXHIBITION – LOWER SCHOOL LIBRARY

The Exhibition will be in Lower School on Friday, Monday and Tuesday, when the organisers will explain the exhibits to one class in each period of those days. A list of the arrangements is given below. The rest of the 2nd Year can see the Exhibition during tutor periods or at lunchtime.

A list of the necessary room changes is given on the Lower School Staff Notice Board.

Friday	Class	Teacher Releasing Class
p.1	1E	Gladys Down
p.2	1L	Pat Evans and Mike Frost
p.3	1P	Kathy Gatting
p.4	1R	Mike Frost
Monday		
p.1	1M	Kathy Gatting
p.2	1A	Phil Abrahams
p.3	1I	Janet Howe
p.4	1D	Gladys Down
Tuesday		
p.1	2I	Kathy Gatting
p.2	2E/L	Pat Irwell
p.3	2A	Anna Jones
p.4	2R	Muriel Kite

6   HEAD OF FACULTY MEETING 25TH JUNE

A Report of this meeting is included as an Appendix to this Bulletin.

7   FROM DAVID LOFTUS (PE) AND MARGARET MADDOCKS (ML)

a)   Industry Year – update

A file has been compiled of local firms and contacts for staff to use. This includes existing contacts, a business directory, staff contacts and firms owned or run by parents of pupils at school.

An offer has recently been made by the local Rotary Club, whose members are keen to be involved in developing links with schools in the area. If you would like to be involved see David Loftus.

A Challenge of Industry Conference has been arranged to take place at **Westcliffe** on the 15th and 16th January 1987. It will be organised by the Industrial Society in conjunction with school. It is an event for all lower sixth formers and its purpose is to bring practising managers and trade unionists into schools, where they can establish contact and provide students with the opportunity to discuss many issues facing industry.

b)   Mini-Co in town

Next year, as an activity within project options, groups of lower sixth students will be taking part in the Mini-Enterprise Scheme. This involves them having to set up and run a company, choosing a product to manufacture, selling to the public, then liquidating the company. They will then count the profit or loss, and hopefully learn from the experience – whatever the result.

In order that the scheme should have the best chance of success, links with local industry will be vital. If you have any contacts in industry with people who would like to establish links with **Westcliffe** in Industry Year, would you please let Margaret or Dave know.

8   IN-SERVICE DAYS – 17TH AND 18TH JULY, 1986

The menus for the In-service days are as follows:

Thursday Ploughman's   Granary roll, butter, cheddar cheese, cottage cheese, salad with pickle. Cheesecake.

Friday   Turkey, jacket potato, butter, salad. Fruit pie and cream.

The meals, for which there will be no charge, will be served in Upper School canteen. If you would like a meal, please let Margaret Battersby know by Friday, 27th June.

9   SPORTS WEEK – FROM TERRY NORTON (H/PE)

Inter-Form Sports Competitions

DATE	MORNING	AFTERNOON
Friday, 4th July	1st Year Swimming	—
Monday, 7th July	4th Year Cricket (Boys) 4th Year Rounders (Girls)	6th Year Special Event 3rd & 4th Year Athletics 1st & 2nd Year Sport Aid Fun Run
	3rd–6th Years – GOLF COMPETITION	
Tuesday, 8th July	3rd Year Cricket (Boys) 3rd Year Rounders (Girls)	2nd Year Cricket (Boys) 2nd Year Rounders (Girls)
Wednesday, 9th July	3rd Year Tennis (Girls)	3rd Year Tennis (Boys)
Thursday, 10th July	1st Year Cricket (Boys) 1st Year Rounders (Girls) 4th Year Tennis (Boys)	1st & 2nd Year Athletics 3rd, 4th & 6th Year Sport Aid Fun Run
Friday, 11th July	2nd Year Swimming Gala 4th Year Tennis (Girls)	

Will staff please note the following:

a) Tutors will be with Tutor groups on Monday and Thursday afternoons. 5th Year tutors will be helping with the Fun Run.

b) At other times, children who are not taking part in the competitions will go to their normal lessons.

c) If you teach 1st years on Friday 4th July (am) or 2nd years on Friday 11th July (am) bring your classes down to the baths for 9.30 or come and collect them from the baths after morning break.

d) If the particular year you teach is involved in cricket/rounders you may bring the children out to watch, but they must remain under your supervision and you must take them back at break.

10 THE LOWER SIXTH – FROM DAVE OWENS (H/MATHS)

During Wednesday, Thursday and Friday of next week, the lower sixth are all off timetable as they will be in the Lake District.

Pupils will be housed at Ambleside Youth Hostel and will take part in a wide variety of activities, including archery, abseiling, assault course, canoeing, horse-riding, sailing and windsurfing. All instruction is by qualified professional instructors. The group will also complete a moderate hike and, for those who opt for it, there will be the opportunity to undertake a more strenuous hike, including camping out at a pre-booked campsite.

Staff involved (who thank you in advance for your co-operation) are D Owens, P Paul, V Quick, C Roper, M Maddocks, R Store and C Tate.

There will be a barbecue on the Thursday evening in the grounds of the Hostel. All staff wishing to visit are more than welcome – but please book with the Sixth Form, that particular venture is organised by them.

11 POOLS – FROM DAVE OWEN (H/MATHS)

Not only are England not going to win the World Cup, but sadly it seems we are still looking for a win. During the Australian season we have reduced our premium and now have about £100 spare. I would like to propose that we invest in some premium bonds with this money (in Registrar's name) and increase our options. If there is general agreement with this idea I will devise a 'set of rules' and circulate to all members of the syndicate (please tell the Registrar if you are in favour). No pools during the summer holiday.

12 CHILD ABUSE

Staff are reminded of the guidance in the 'Handbook of Procedures' (15/1/5/83) which indicates the action to be taken when child abuse is suspected. Copies of this handbook are kept in the Head's room and in my room.

13 FROM THE LEA EDUCATION NEWSLETTER OF 20.6.86

SECURITY-UNAUTHORISED ACCESS

Headteachers are advised that the man described in Newsletter 30, 2nd May and Newsletter 33, 6th June '86 is still visiting schools. Reports have been received of two further intruders of a similar nature and descriptions of all three are detailed below.

1 Man, 5'8" tall – ginger to dark-coloured short hair, with fringe, short ginger beard, slim build and well dressed in tan leather jacket and blue/grey trousers.

2 Man, age 20–25 – pockmarked face with prominently decaying teeth, black beard and black curly hair. Wearing brown and tan checked shirt and blue jeans. This man gives an address and refers to a sister named Anne Marie with a daughter named Diane, as part of his story.

3 Man, swarthy complexion, light hair, no beard. 5'8" tall – slim build. This man asks for details of day nurseries in the area as part of his story.

Headteachers are asked to telephone the Police Communication Centre immediately, should they receive a visit from any of these persons and to notify, subsequently, the office services section ext.

Ref: Office Services ext.

BOYS' AND GIRLS' WELFARE SOCIETY

A teacher (scale 1+SSA) part-time or full-time, is required at Herod's School, for September 1986.

Herod's is a school for physically handicapped children of secondary age (11–19). The person appointed will be expected to teach science throughout the school, and prepare small groups of children for the new GCSE in 1988. The school has a fully equipped science laboratory.

Application forms and further particulars are available from the Headteacher.

BOOKS SURPLUS TO REQUIREMENTS

The Rotary Club is again asking Headteachers if they have any books of any description, that are surplus to the school's requirements. Last year over 5,000 books were collected from local schools and sent out as libraries to schools in the Third World.

Headteachers are asked to contact Brian Young if they have any surplus books available from their school. All books will be collected on Wednesday, 23rd July.

Ref: Brian Young.

OPEN UNIVERSITY COURSES

Arrangements are being made within the Open University to take up places on the following four nationally recognised courses:

E323	Management and the School
E333	Policy-making in Education
EP851	Applied Studies in Educational Management
PME233	Mathematics Across the Curriculum

The courses will run from February to October 1986 and all count towards diplomas.

Teachers interested in taking one of these courses are invited to attend a meeting at the Centre on Tuesday, 15th July, commencing at 4.15 pm, when further details will be given. Any teacher unable to come on that occasion but who would like to reserve a place on a course should write to Mr D Zimnock, Education Adviser.

It would be appreciated if Headteachers would draw attention to this meeting at an appropriate staff meeting.

14   SCHOOL BAND – FROM REG UNWIN (H/MUSIC)
On Thursday, 3rd July, Band practice will start at 2.35 pm instead of the usual 3.45 pm. This is to enable the Band to rehearse their full programme of music for the forthcoming School Concert on 15th July.

It would be appreciated if members of staff could excuse 'Bandpersons' from lesson 4 on that date. The players will approach you personally to ask permission and will have with them proof of Band membership!

15   FROM THE REGISTRAR

Missing: One set of Minibus Keys – would staff please check pockets, handbags, etc.

16   FROM JOHN VARLEY (ART TEACHER)

Apologies for missing Home Economics off my discussion document in last week's Bulletin – I am duly chastened!

17   COMPUTER STUDIES

Any member of staff who would like to teach 2 periods of Computer Studies next year should contact David Owens immediately.

© Derek Torrington, Jane Weightman, Basil Blackwell Ltd, 1989.

18   LEA M, B, C, MOTOR CAR ALLOWANCES

Please note that with effect from 1st May, car mileage allowances were revised as follows:

Casual User Allowances

Miles per annum	451–999 cc	1000–1199cc	1200–1450cc	1451–1750cc
0–1500	30.3p	33.1p	38.6p	42.5p
1501–5500	21.3p	23.4p	27.0p	29.7p
5501–11000	16.4p	18.1p	20.6p	22.7p
after 11000	7.8p	8.9p	9.6p	10.4p
Amount of VAT per mile in petrol element	0.554p	0.599p	0.633p	0.693p

Essential User Allowance

	451–999 cc	1000–1199cc	1200–1450cc	1451–1750cc
Lump sum per annum	£405	£438	£522	£579
Per mile – first 11,000 miles	16.4p	18.1p	20.6p	22.7p
Per mile after 11,000 miles	7.8p	8.9p	9.6p	10.4p
Amount of VAT per mile in petrol element	0.554p	0.599p	0.633p	0.693p

19   FOR SALE

From Margaret Wilson (Special Ed Teacher): Shrinking family (on holidays) forces us to sell our large French GIFACO frame tent – 6-7 berth, chocolate brown and cream colour. Three large bedroom compartments with sewn-in groundsheet. Opening front and sides for heatwaves! Super tent for large family or small family with lots of friends, or just those who like 5-star camping for four! Good condition – may be seen erected. £170 o.n.o.

From Doris Young (Registrar): Gold Mazda Hatchback. August 1982 'Y' Reg. Cavity-sealed, one driver from new. 27,000 miles only. Radio/stereo cassette. Genuine reason for sale. Superb car. £2,100.

20   TAILPIECE

Comment by a lady (not Jean – Head's Secretary!) overheard by the Head in his secretary's office:

'You have to take your clothes off to enjoy it.'

Appendix: Heads of Faculty Meeting: 25.6.86

Present: Barry (Chair), Max (Minutes), David, Roger, Julie, Mike, Tony, David (HT).

Apologies: Terry

1 Calendar

The idea of, for example, a mathematics 'experience' rather than a field course or educational visit for a particular year group, was floated. No objections were raised but it was suggested that it might best take place alongside Sports Week or at that time of the summer term.

The idea of the mathematics staff, particularly applied statisticians, joining the Biology field trip in an advisory capacity, was also discussed and given a cautious welcome by Dave.

2 Staff Development/INSET

Discussion took place only briefly, the matter being discussed at length later in the meeting.

Report from the meeting between Heads and the Director

a) Because of the quickening administrative tempo within the Authority, there is a need for the Head to inform and consult with Heads of Faculty immediately following the now regular meetings with the Director. This was accepted and welcomed by Heads of Faculty.

b) Items from the latest meeting (24.6.86):
(i)   The 'ring' fence still exists for secondary appointments.
(ii)   Concern exists over the slow progress made by the reorganisation working parties.
(iii)   The redeployment arrangements are in some disarray.
(iv)   Arrangements for absence from work, particularly without pay, are to be reviewed.
(v)   There is concern over the continuing provision of school nurses and the way they are appointed.
(vi)   Midday-supervision: the Education Committee has approved a scheme to provide midday supervisors which all teachers' associations reject.
(vii)   The printing unit at the Teachers' Centre is to be moved to the Town Hall Print Unit. Primary schools which used to use the Teachers' Centre will make use of facilities in local secondary schools.
(viii) An attempt to increase use of the IBM terminals in schools will be made. PCs may be offered as 'sweeteners'.

(ix)   An increasing amount of financial delegation to schools is likely in the near future. Virement between areas of expenditure is to be part of the system.

c) TRIST

It now seems to be accepted by the Authority's officers that the LEA has been very much 'out of step' with other Authorities inasmuch as it has used TRIST finance to support off-site training rather than school-based initiatives. As the latter assume their correct importance the onus will be on schools to define their own priorities and press their claims for support.

The importance and urgency of the request re INSET in the Staff Bulletin of 19.6.86 should now be apparent. The school will make an outline submission in July and a more detailed one after staff have played their part in formulating and prioritising needs during the September INSET.

d) GCSE: There are now four sources of finance:
(i)   £3,074 as allocated by the Authority earlier in the year as 'pump priming'.
(ii)   A package approved by the Education Committee (but awaiting full Council endorsement) as follows:
        £21,000 for consumables
        £20,000 for new equipment
        5% increase in ancillary provision
        An increase of at least 15 FTE teaching staff
(iii)   £15M from DES, £5M from MSC (January or later) – as announced by the new Minister earlier this month.
(iv)   £20M already promised by the government (April 1987 and after).

It was agreed to distribute the sum under (i) above on a per capita basis between Faculties. When Faculties were in a better position to assess their needs and when the amounts actually become available to the school under (ii), (iii) and (iv) above, allocation of the further sums could be discussed.

With regard to the July INSET, two points were made. First, the onus is on individual schools to assess their needs and organise programmes (ie little help will be forthcoming from the advisory service), and second, the way is open for Departments/Faculties to co-operate with those in other schools.

Finally, it was agreed to meet again on Wednesday, 9th July at 12 noon in Special Education.

Max
25.6.86

> **STAFF BULLETIN**
>
> **HALL END**
>
> **TUESDAY, 23rd SEPTEMBER 1986**

1 NEW PUPILS YEAR 4

Eileen Alcot – 4 Orange

Maths Set 5	Teacher's name
English	Teacher's name
Option A	Social Studies
B	Biology
C	Textiles
D	Drama
E	English Literature

Philip Bowden – 4 Silver

Maths Set 5	Teacher's name
English	Teacher's name
Option A	Geography
B	Biology
C	CDT
D	Engineering Technology
E	Art

G. T. Clarke (DHT)

2 CONFERENCE REPORTS

The following reports have been lodged in the Staff Resources Room.

(1) RE's contribution to Personal and Social Education in the Secondary School. DES Course No. 777 re – 18th July 1986.

(2) Section 11 Seminar 10th September 1986.

D. Davies (HT)

3 CAREERS ROOM

Would Upper School tutors inform their tutor groups that the careers office in Upper School dining room will be open each Monday and Tuesday between 3.30 pm and 4.00 pm. Thank you.

C. Eccles (H/Careers)

© Derek Torrington, Jane Weightman, Basil Blackwell Ltd, 1989.

4   NEW PUPIL YEAR 5 SILVER

Carol Franks

Maths Group 4	Teacher's name
English	
Option A	Child Care
B	Environmental Studies
C	Biology
D	F.D.F.
E	Office Practice

G. Clarke (DHT)

5   INSET

These courses are being run by the Development Unit and will be extremely useful for all curricular/pastoral areas. I would recommend early enquiry and application. If you have any questions concerning the course ring and ask for Christine or Ruth.

Practical approaches to assessment

A series of three workshop sessions to consider internal assessment issues and techniques which will be of use to primary and lower school secondary teachers.

Numbers are restricted to 30. Please telephone or write to the Unit to book a place.

Venue	Teachers' Centre
Course Tutor	Ruth
Dates	Thursday, 20th November 4.30–6.00 – Hut A
	Thursday, 27th November 4.30–6.00 – Hut A
	Thursday, 4th December 4.30–6.00 – Room 24

Reviewing

A three-session course for teachers and lecturers to look at the reviewing process as part of learning and profiling. There will be opportunities to practise the skills of reviewing in each session. In addition teachers will be able to reflect on and review their own careers whilst developing the skills appropriate to use with students. Are you fully aware of your strengths and how to use them, either for career development or job fulfilment? This review may help teachers set targets for professional and staff development. In addition, there will be some input on writing a curriculum vitae if teachers wish to produce a cv as an end product of their review. Professional and personal information shared will be regarded as confidential to the course.

Places are limited to 30 and are only available to teachers who can attend all three sessions as the progression is important. Please contact the Unit to book a place.

Venue	Teachers' Centre
Course Tutors	Moira – Central College Christine
Dates	Tuesday, 4th November 6.30–8.30 Room 24 Tuesday, 11th November 6.30–8.30 Room 24 Tuesday, 18th November 6.30–8.30 Room 24

'Current Approaches to Assessment and Accreditation'

A series of free-standing seminars to provide basic information on key developments. Please contact the Unit to book places. Numbers are limited to 40. All sessions are held at the Teachers' Centre.

Thursday, 25th September
4.30–6.30 Room 18

Ruth 'Common Themes in Current Developments – An overview'

Thursday, 2nd October
4.30–6.30 Room 24

Dud 'NPRA Unit Credit'

Thursday, 9th October
4.30–6.30 Room 24

Jerry 'GCSE and Modular GCSE'

Thursday, 23rd October

Ruth 'Records of Achievement – an Accumulating Portfolio'

'NPRA Unit Credit – Writing Workshops'

Venue	Teachers' Centre
Course Tutor	Dud
Dates	Thursday, 6th November 7.00–9.00 – Room 24 Thursday, 13th November 7.00–9.00 – Room 24 Thursday, 20th November 7.00–9.00 – Room 24 Thursday, 27th November 7.00–9.00 – Room 24

Unit Credits are gaining in popularity and use throughout the LEA's schools and colleges. You can develop the skills you need, or 'check up' on the units you have already written by dropping in at any time to the Teachers' Centre between 7.00–9.00 pm on the dates above.

M. Stott (TVEI Profiles)

6   OPTION CHANGE – 4 E

Scott Howard from Control Technology to English Literature – Parental Request.

G. Clarke (DHT)

7   MEDICAL EXAMINATION (4th Year)

The following 4th Year pupils are to attend the medical suite on Wednesday morning at the times indicated:

9.30	10.00
Three names	Two names

10.30	11.00
Two names	Two names

G. Thrace (i/c Child Care)

8   DUTY TEAM – TUESDAY 8.50, 10.10, 3.30

Team Leader   J. Clare (H/CDT)
Upper School
    Right of Way   G. Thrace
    Entrance   R. Abrams (H/Eng)
    M10 Area   A. Jones (H/Art)
    Top Floor   D. McGuire (H/Y3)

Playground
Lower School
    Entrance   P. Singh
    Right of Way   M. Tinker
    L/S Steps   H. Trout

Senior Staff   D. Bird (DHT)

G. Clarke (DHT)

9   VARIATIONS TO TIMETABLE/OUTSIDE VISITS

May I remind staff that any variations to timetable must be agreed through the proper system. Permission to take groups out of school must be obtained beforehand, even when the activity takes place within a timetabled lesson and doesn't cut across other lessons. The system of gaining Head of Department support, Head of School/Deputy Head support as appropriate, and finally Headteacher's approval *must be followed*, using the revised green form (ref: AMAD 1).

D. Davies (HT)

10   RELEASE FROM LESSONS AT 12.30 pm

I apologise in advance to those staff for whom the following remarks are not needed.

A large number of pupils were released before the end of lesson 3. The problem was:

(i)   whole classes released early;

(ii)   pupils sent to return books who then had time on their hands without an instruction to return to the lesson.

It is the responsibility of members of staff to supervise their classes for the whole of the lesson. There is no supervision at the dining room until 12.30 pm. Staff **must** ensure that they take responsibility for their class for the whole of the lesson.

Orderly release from lessons

The 12.30 bell is a signal to staff that pupils may be dismissed if staff are ready to dismiss them. It is not a signal for a general charging out into the corridor before the bell has even stopped ringing, followed by a race down the corridors and stairs to get into the dinner queue. I would ask that classes are dismissed when the bell has ceased ringing. We have a responsibility for ensuring that dismissal is orderly and if necessary must take appropriate action if it is clear that our classes do not behave well after leaving our lesson. I respectfully suggest that one can usually see before dismissal what the situation is likely to be. *The first step to take is to stand at the door when the class is dismissed and observe the movement in the corridor. If all staff do this we will put a stop to the problem.*

I repeat: apologies to those staff for whom these messages are not needed.

D. Davies (HT)

11 DUTY TEAMS – AUTUMN 1986/87

In an attempt to spread duty to days when staff have not got a full day's teaching commitment, I am suggesting a modified rota to come into operation on Monday, 29 September.

Upper School	Monday	Tuesday	Wednes-day	Thursday	Friday
Team leader	D	J	C	G	R
Right of way	A	G	R	D	S
Entrance/ boys' toilets	B	J	M	G	P
Dining room/ library M11	J	AL	AD	R	J
Top floor	E	C	EM	P	AY
Leisure centre		M			
Music/Drama area		X-Music			
Lower School	Monday	Tuesday	Wednes-day	Thursday	Friday
Entrance	S	P	A	M	P
Steps	P	M	H	S	A
Right of way	G	P	C	D	S
Senior Staff	M	D	C	G	L

G. Clarke (DHT)

12 Senior management teams: finding cohesion and purpose

Work on the materials in this chapter should not be undertaken without being quite sure that the participants are ready to cope with the fundamental issues that it involves. It is intended as an intensive programme of work by all the members of a senior team in a school to clarify each of their roles and to ensure that all of them have a 'real' job to do. It takes at least eight hours to work through the exercise satisfactorily, so it is most appropriate for a weekend away, where the work can be interspersed with opportunities for relaxation and informal conversation.

On completion of the exercise participants should be able to:

a) define a clear role and purpose for their management job;
b) understand the roles and purpose of their senior colleagues;
c) consult with other colleagues in the school about the school mission and how its objectives are to be achieved.

Participants will need:
Senior Team Document I – *The powerful Head*
Senior Team Document II – *Ronald's job description*
Senior Team Document III – *90 minutes in Ronald's day*
Senior Team Document IV – *Maureen's duties*
Senior Team Document V – *Maureen's morning*
Senior Team Document VI – *Heads and Deputies: a point of view*
Senior Team Document VII – *The effective Head*

To the trainer

This exercise is designed for an intensive examination of the roles, expectations and contribution of the various members of the senior team in a school. Ideally the group should be small, and Head and Deputies is the most appropriate. Adding in other senior staff could jeopardise the venture unless all participants are genuinely sharing the central task of managing the school. It is not suggested that governors should be included, as the focus is on the detailed interaction of full-time professionals, rather than on more general strategic issues.

The role and position of Deputy Heads cannot be understood in isolation from their particular Head, on whom they are dependent to a much greater degree than almost any other member of school. Also, one cannot envisage Headship in the future being a coherent, 'do-able' job unless Deputies share that unique responsibility in a more sensible way than is now common. The demands on secondary comprehensive schools are so great and diverse, and come from so many sources, that the only reasonable prospect of being successful in the future lies with some reconstruction of the traditional Head/Deputies relationship. For too long Deputies have been cast in the role of occasional substitutes for, or regular assistants and support to, the Head. Now they need to take on major responsibilities of their own, and this requires not only that Heads more willingly share the duties of Headship, but that Deputies create an independent meaning and purpose in their jobs to an extent that has previously been unusual.

In British schools there is an almost universal focus on the job of Headteacher as being the pivot of all management and organisation. This is found not only in the work of academics such as, for example, Rutter (1979) and Mortimore (1988), but also in the continuing statements of politicians. This centrality of the Headteacher puzzles those outside education:

> When comparing the organization of secondary schools with the organization of most other employing organizations, the position of the Head is almost unique in the power vested in it. The Headteacher is the leading figure in an organization employing somewhere between 50 and 125 people. Those people, plus the parents of the children in the school, plus the children themselves, the school governors and the local authority administrators all seem anxious that the Headteacher should be kept remote and should exercise considerable power. Very rarely will any member of the staff address him by his first name. Although there may be consultation, it is expected that the Head will personally resolve major aspects of school policy. When Subject Heads decide who shall teach their subject at different levels, these decisions only have the status of recommendations that the Head may well change as he, and he alone, has effective authority in relation to members of staff.
>
> (Torrington and Weightman, 1985, p. 199)

And two pages later . . .

> Effective delegation is essential, but the power assumptions about the role of the Headteacher are so deep-rooted that the delegation is difficult to contrive.
>
> (*ibid*. p. 201)

The most recent empirical study of Headteachers is by Hall, Mackay and Morgan (1986) who studied the working lives of 15 Headteachers and found them to differ widely; all could be characterised, however, by fragmentation, a wide variety of tasks and a strong emphasis on talking to people. In many ways this coincides closely with studies of general managers in commercial organisations, but it also demonstrates that there is no consensus on what the job of Headteacher consists of. The authors decry the lack of 'the baseline of a formal description'. Since the Hall, Mackay and Morgan research, there has been the development of the new contracts for members of the teaching profession, but these are very broad guidelines and Headteachers remain free to organise their jobs in almost any way they choose. It is sad that the Hall study shows many Heads to be at the mercy of events, responding to every problem as important and involved in mainly trivial matters. That type of reactive, rudderless approach has inescapable implications for everyone else, for example:

> ... each Head's style of working with staff was significantly tied to the kind of relationship they had with senior staff; and the extent to which they had consciously instituted systems into the school management structure for ensuring tasks were carried out.
>
> (Hall, Mackay and Morgan, 1986, p. 206)

Two of the Heads in the study seemed to have developed a meaningful role for Deputies, despite contrasted approaches to the job of Headship. First Mr Dowe:

> He preferred a collegial rather than hierarchical approach to staff relations. The extent of his availability to staff, to whom he was always considerate and respectful, was curtailed by his extensive teaching and examining commitments ... He sought to demonstrate through his own professional competence as a teacher the ways in which he wanted staff to see their own teaching roles ... he delegated running the school extensively. As a result he was required to spend relatively little time in dealing with matters requiring immediate attention; his teaching commitments dominated the space available.
>
> (*ibid.* p. 210)

Mr Shaw interpreted his job differently, emphasising his leading professional role more generally in school affairs, but there was still a significant enablement of Deputies:

> The main features ... were his systematic involvement in the whole range of the school's activity, in spite of extensive commitments to activities outside the school; his strategic view of school matters, ensuring continuing attention to longer-term planning; and his proactive stance towards innovation and change ... he approached systematically the task of building and maintaining interpersonal relations with staff, pupils

and parents; as well as creating mechanisms for providing staff with the knowledge and skills to do their job effectively. He did this by involving staff consistently in the school's decision-making processes, making extensive use of his close working relationship with his senior management team to secure the staff's support.

(ibid. p. 211)

Setting the management work of the Head in the context of all the management work done within the school suggests a need to reappraise the taken-for-granted view that Headteachers have to be strong leaders.

Deputy Headteachers, in contrast, have the least clearly defined jobs in schools. Their work varies enormously both within and between schools, but many are essentially personal assistants to the Headteacher rather than senior staff with clear and significant responsibilities justifying their status and salary. With most schools having three such posts, it is clear that not all will become Heads. Being a Deputy is the opportunity for some to be a 'Head-in-waiting', but for many others it is their final post. If these people do not have whole and coherent jobs to do they will become fed up; their enthusiasm blunted. The Head loses an opportunity to shed some of the workload of Headship and other staff resent the privileged position of people whose extra contribution they cannot see.

The powerful Head

Distribute copies of Document I and get the group to work through a series of questions:

1 What would you see as the benefits of this Headteacher's power to:
   - the school as a whole
   - the children
   - the staff in general
   - the senior team
2 Are there any drawbacks for any of those four?
3 In what ways would a Peter Ford-type Head be suitable (and in what ways unsuitable) for your school?

Discussion round these questions could be aided by the following ideas, as well as the material on the MOSS quadrants in Part III of this book:

Powerful Heads can create several problems within the school

First, if all decisions and systems depend on the Head there is a vacuum when they are absent. For example, in Peter Ford's school the senior staff were reluctant to take decisions when he was absent, as the decision would frequently be reversed when he returned.

Second, staff cannot develop beyond a mediocre level without becoming a serious challenge to a powerful Head. They are restricted by needing to behave in acceptable ways and have congruent ideas and approaches.

Third, in two schools we visited that had very powerful Heads the staff had formalised their union activities so that their views could be expressed within the school. Both these Heads were national figures, and their personal dominance had produced such social distance between themselves and the rest of the staff that the culture of the school was impaired.

Fourth, the school tends to reflect the weaknesses as well as the strengths of the Head.

Fifth, it is becoming increasingly impracticable for one person to encompass the diversity and volume of work necessary to manage and organise a secondary school.

These five aspects suggest that a powerful Head can only take their school so far in development; there is a limit on the capacity for commitment and self-renewing. There is no doubt that strong leaders can recover difficult situations as Peter Ford had done in coping with the aftermath of two schools being amalgamated, but they need to change as time passes. Also there is a shortage of powerful Heads who are competent. Peter Ford was very successful in many ways and attracted the enthusiastic support of his staff. Other Heads operate in a similar centralised way without having the personal qualities 'to get away with it', so that the whole school is disabled by a power structure without effective power.

Document VII is an example of an effective Head who empowered his Deputies. It may be useful as a background to discussion drawing out the differences.

The powerless Deputy

Here we have two different sorts of evidence; first the evidence of the job description for the position Ronald held; second the evidence from our observation of how he spent his time.

1 Distribute Document II and invite comments on it. The following ideas may help discussion:

Initially this job description may seem to be full of substance and variety, with a wide range of interesting duties. Closer inspection shows it to be characterised by imprecision and a lack of wholeness. It does not describe a job but is a rambling list of odds and ends.

Furthermore only (8), (12) and (13) are specific duties that stand on their own; all the others are supporting, assisting, liaising or in some way dependent on someone else to share their work.

Some of the shortcomings are:

(1) 'To deputise for the Headteacher as required.' This is a general-purpose availability to fill in for the Head. It is undoubtedly necessary, but its only significance is the status it clearly confers on the holder.

(3a) 'Supporting form tutors and year heads in their pastoral work.' A statement so vague as to be unhelpful to everyone involved. There is no clear delineation of the sort of support to be provided, nor what should be withheld to avoid infringing the proper responsibility of form tutors. The result is that tutors expect support on some matters but don't get it and feel they are overseen on matters where supervision is irrelevant.

(3f) 'Assisting with the conduct of external examinations.' Assisting whom? In what way?

(5) 'To have a knowledge of the school-based and external careers guidance available to pupils.' Does this knowledge get used? How?

2 Now distribute Document III. Allow ten minutes for members of the group to read it.

3 Invite comments on Ronald's duties. (If necessary, remind team members of the sTAMp method of analysis described in Part I of this book.) Ronald himself regarded the period of observation as typical. Comment by the researchers who conducted the observation is as follows:

> We do not suggest that all these duties are unimportant: we assert emphatically that most of them are a waste of an experienced, highly-paid teacher. The fact that they are undertaken by a **Deputy Head** teacher is almost beyond belief. What is also beyond belief is that the school's Head is seriously over-burdened with responsibilities.

22% of Ronald's day was spent on technical work, 22% on administrative work, 28% on managerial work, and 24% was personal.

The effective Deputy

Maureen is an example of how a Deputy Head made sure she had a real job to do. Emphasise that *she* made sure; it was not simply conferred upon her. Distribute Document IV. The following may help discussion:

Maureen works in the same school as Daniel (see Document VII), with the title of Deputy Head (Administration and Staff Support). This gives her a role very similar to that of a personnel manager. In the staff handbook she is shown as being responsible for the duties described in Document IV.

She sees her main tasks as staff development and anti-racism (which includes links with the community). The administrative aspects of her role she accepts as involving important things that have to be done promptly and efficiently, but they are jobs to get done rather than jobs to make the most of. She delegates as much of the clerical work as possible to non-teaching and teaching colleagues.

She explains her relationship with the Head:

> 'I have links – if I pick up disturbing or important signals I take them to him. It may irritate him because I'm telling him things he doesn't want to hear, but he appreciates the need for consultation. I like working with him as I believe we have a constructive working relationship. I will see him about areas of concern and tell him what I think. On many matters we're opposed, but we try to use those differences of perspective to get the best possible understanding of a question and a balanced resolution: it's not power games. We are the buffer between two pressures on the school – the community and the LEA – and our contrasted views help us make the buffer effective.'

Maureen's list of jobs could potentially be no better than Ronald's. However, the words liaise, assist, support do not appear and are not generally implicit, although there are duties that are explicitly shared with others. There are a number of specific but significant responsibilities that give Maureen the scope to develop her duties into a major contribution to the school and a personally satisfying, demanding job.

Distribute Document V. Typical of Maureen's day was the fact that it was organised by her into discrete parts. Document V gives the details of the morning. Compared with Ronald there are fewer interruptions and less flitting from item to item. Perhaps most noticeable are the large amounts of time spent doing managerial work. Typical of these are the discussions with heads of department about departmental effectiveness, discussing with the probationer her performance, and with a community leader the needs of his members. Maureen's personal skill in handling these events made for useful exchanges with all participants, despite some heads of department finding aspects of the questioning awkward.

Policy and roles

Members of the group now need to turn their discussion and analysis to their own situation, considering their demands, choices and constraints and how duties and responsibilities should be divided between them. It is suggested that there should be a break after the previous phases and before beginning this phase, so that participants have an opportunity to consolidate what they have learned so far, and are refreshed for the searching (and possibly threatening) analysis that is to come.

Take the school mission statement or policy statement on aims and objectives, and use brainstorming methods to develop (on a flip chart) a series of lists:

1 The main challenges facing the school in the next five years.
2 Ways in which we really ought to develop the mission further in that period.
3 Other ways in which we would like to develop the mission in that period, if we could.
4 A ranked list of tasks that we feel we could accomplish.
5 Provisional 'agendas' (see Part I of this book) involved by the ranked list.

Roles and responsibilities

Now ask the group to consider how each member will develop their role as part of the senior management team in the whole school staff. Distribute Document VI and allow ten minutes for this to be read. Then develop the discussion around it. The document describes a point of view held by the authors of this book after completing their research. It is neither 'right' nor 'wrong': it is an informed judgement reached by people outside school management after careful consideration.

Questions for consideration:

1 What points in this document do we agree with?
2 With which points do we disagree?
   (It is unlikely that there will be unanimity in the answers to both questions. Minority views need to be discussed and understood as well as the general consensus.)
3 What are the reasons for our disagreement with the authors' views?
   • Is it that our experience tells us better?
   • Does our situation in this school make us different?
   • Is there something about us as a group which makes the analysis inappropriate?

4 What is our collective view about the nature of the working relationship between each of us, especially the different levels of responsibility to be held by Heads, Deputies and senior teachers?
5 What is our collective view about the nature of the working relationship, and the different levels of responsibility, between ourselves and head of faculty, department, year and so on?
6 Do our answers to questions 4 and 5 represent the most sensible and effective distribution so as to make the best use of all the talents available in the school?

Jobs

The last main stage of this exercise is to examine the jobs of each member of the team in the light of the foregoing analysis. The method is for each member to write, or review, his or her own job description so as to set up for the future an arrangement whereby the agreed mission for the future will be carried through by a group of people who are not only committed to the mission, but who have also worked out a share of work and responsibility between them that will bind them together as an efficient and harmonious working team.

1 Each member produces a personal job description that describes how that person visualises working through his or her appropriate portion of the work the senior team has to undertake.
2 The job descriptions are copied and distributed so that everyone has a copy of each for study and comparison.
3 The group collectively discuss all the descriptions;
   - to see what jobs have been omitted. These are listed on a flip chart.
   - to see where there is duplication or lack of clear responsibility. These are also listed.
   - to examine each description in turn to see the extent to which it describes a satisfactory job that can be done, asking the job holder for reservations about any area, or ways in which the job could be improved.
   - to see if the jobs collectively make sense, are compatible and represent the most effective distribution of responsibility and exploitation of expertise.

This discussion has to continue until all are convinced of and committed to the roles of themselves and each other.

Consultation and dissemination

The final task for the group is to decide what consultation there should be with other members of the school to make sure necessary modifications are made: a) because of the limited knowledge of the senior team; b) to win the commitment of colleagues.

References

Adams, P, 'Time's Up', in *Times Educational Supplement*, 29th July, 1988.

Burns, M, *Leadership*, Harper and Row, 1978.

Hall, V, Mackay, H and Morgan, C, *Headteachers at Work*, Open University Press, 1986.

HMI, *Ten Good Schools*, DES/HMSO, 1977.

Hodgkinson, C, *The Philosophy of Leadership*, Blackwell, Oxford, 1953.

Hoyle, E, *The Politics of School Management*, Hodder and Stoughton, 1986.

Peters, TJ and Waterman RH, *In Search of Excellence*, Harper and Row, New York, 1982.

Mortimore, P, Sammons, P, Stoll, L, Lewis, D and Ecob, R, *School Matters: The Junior Years*, Open Books, 1988.

Reid, P, 'Hours not to reason why', in *Times Educational Supplement*, 8th January, 1988.

Rutter, M, et al *1500 Hours*, Penguin, 1979.

Selznick, P, *Leadership in Administration*, Harper and Row, New York, 1957.

Sergiovanni, TJ, 'Cultural and competing perspectives in administrative theory and practice', in Sergiovanni, TJ and Corbally, JE, *Leadership and Organizational Culture*, University of Illinois Press, Urbana, 1984.

Torrington, DP and Weightman, JB, 'Teachers and the Management Trap', *Journal of Curriculum Studies*, Vol. 17, No. 21, pp. 197–205, 1985.

Torrington, DP and Weightman, JB, *The Reality of School Management*, Basil Blackwell, 1989.

Torrington, DP, Weightman, JB and Johns K, 'Doing well: could do better', in *Times Educational Supplement*, 30th October, 1987.

Weightman, JB, 'The Balance of Work for Senior Staff in Schools', *School Organisation*, 1989.

Senior team Document I: The powerful Head

The Head, Peter Ford, was universally respected and admired by the staff in the school. Such words as 'fantastic', 'exceptional', 'outstanding' were frequently used. He was also seen as powerful and influential, the phrase 'The Peter Ford Show' occurring time and again.

There were five distinct sources of this power:

1 The traditional *position* of Headteachers. The near-universal view is that Headteachers should be strong leaders, so that those holding the position automatically assume the power that others vest in it. This is demonstrated, for example, in *Ten Good Schools*, which remains a highly regarded treatise 12 years after its first publication. This position power is also sustained by the law, by political pronouncements, and by all those having dealings with the school and therefore wanting a single channel of authority – parents, local authority officials, governors and union representatives.

2 *Historical* factors. The Headteacher had set up the present school 12 years ago, following reorganisation. He had been there from the beginning. During the initial years, policy decisions were required on everything from mixed ability to school uniform. He had an approach of 'Board and Working Party', which meant that most staff had been involved somewhere in deciding school policy. 1974 was also the heyday of teachers' pay, in the wake of the Houghton award, with new salary grades and large salary increases, as well as plenty of money for development and equipment. This was clearly a period of great excitement in the school, following the amalgamation of an apparently depressed boys' secondary modern and a girls' secondary modern. This time was frequently referred to in interviews, perhaps summed up by a shared memory of a golden weekend in St Annes-on-Sea. The Head was seen as the person who had made this happen.

3 *Individual loyalty*. The Headteacher was given loyalty by many individual members of staff following various acts of personal consideration. Many believed they had been promoted further than they would have thought possible because of his encouragement and persuasion – this was a comment only heard from women teachers. Many gave examples of personal consideration shown by the Headteacher over domestic problems and crises, one summed it up by saying, 'He makes it clear that our personal lives are important and should come first'. This was

valued and appeared not to be abused. The Head was seen as approachable on matters both large and small. He had a clearly-stated policy of playing to people's strengths. This was seen to be in effect through the staff development procedures and by the encouragement given to individuals to seek responsibility.

4 *Information.* The Headteacher was involved in various national bodies as well as various local organisations. This ensured he always had the latest information and ideas. He used this information to good effect by making powerful presentations to meetings such as Heads of Faculty, or the Senior Management Group and sharing the information quickly with colleagues: he was both a source of new information and someone willing to share it.

5 The *Senior Management Group* (SMG). The SMG were charged with seeing to all the administrative, individual, day-to-day variations. Great efforts were made by the Headteacher to ensure the SMG were a cohesive group. SMG meetings were held every Wednesday after school when each member described and discussed little items that had come up in the week. These meetings were to ensure a corporate, Medusa-like body that could act as one in all dealings with the staff, no matter who a member of school saw. It would also be quite difficult for any member of SMG to build their own empire within the school when there was such a strong emphasis on 'SMG' as a single entity. All but one had rooms on one corridor, and tasks would be assigned to 'a member of SMG' without an individual being specified. This enabled the Headteacher to be powerful in two ways: first, he was not involved in the daily detail, decisions on which so often irritate those lower in the hierarchy; second, on his own repeated admission, he was protected from the loneliness of Headship by having a cohesive group to support him.

Senior team Document II: Ronald's job description

1 To deputise for the Headteacher as required.

2 To have a general responsibility for all aspects of safety, progress, discipline and pastoral care towards all pupils in the school.

3 As Head of Upper School to have particular responsibility for the pupils in Years IV and V. This responsibility will include:
a) Supporting Form Tutors and Year Heads in their pastoral work.
b) Contact with parents in matters concerning welfare, progress and discipline of pupils.
c) Liaison with external support services.
d) Oversight of the preparation of homework, timetables, pupil reports and records.
e) Assisting Heads of Year in the organisation of Parents' Evenings and Assemblies.
f) Assisting with the conduct of external examinations.
g) Providing general support to the work of the Heads of Year.

4 To liaise with Heads of Year and Head of Lower School regarding mid-year admissions.

5 To have a knowledge of the school-based and external careers guidance available to pupils.

6 To be responsible for the Vocational Links Curriculum as it affects the school.

7 To have oversight of the Health and Safety at Work Provisions and to liaise with the Health and Safety Representatives at school.

8 To deal with all matters concerning repair and maintenance of the campus.

9 To have regular contact with the Caretaking Staff regarding matters affecting the school building and to interview/appoint caretakers/cleaners.

10 To contact Police and Travel Companies as and when necessary.

11 Together with the Heads of Year to deal with matters relating to the suspension or exclusion of pupils.

12 To take assemblies.

13 To carry a teaching load.

14 To undertake other duties as may be detailed by the Headteacher from time to time.

Senior team Document III: 90 minutes in Ronald's day

9.58   Deputy Head in his office. Head of Boys' PE asks him to talk to two boys who he has caught leaving a French lesson early. Head of PE explains that he would have taken boys to Head of Fourth Year if he had been available.

9.59   Boys left outside room. The Deputy Head continues telling the researcher about the school's problems with an external support agency.

10.05   Boys are brought into the room and told off by the Deputy Head.

10.09   Boys leave. Deputy Head talks to the researcher about the position of Modern Languages in his school.

10.14   To the staffroom where he chats to the washing-up lady and then to the researcher. He explains that he always has a cup of tea before break begins so that he can be on duty at break.

10.30   Returns to his office.

10.31   Tells a boy to see a teacher.

10.32   Tells some girls about new bus times.

10.34   Stands around outside room 'on duty'.

10.35   Passing comment to a teacher in the corridor.

10.35   One of the (10.05) boys tells him that he has apologised to the French teacher.

10.36   A boy returns 50p to him.

10.36   He asks a girl to move away from a painting.

10.37   Boy asks if he can fetch a bag.

10.38   Chats affably to a group of girls about their cookery lessons.

10.40   Picks up a plastic bag on floor. Asks a boy to fetch the girl who has dropped it.

10.41   Talks to girl who dropped the plastic bag.

10.42   Talks to two boys.

10.43   Talks to some other boys about bus times.

10.45   Returns to own office.

10.46   Talks to Head of Fourth Year about boys who skipped French.

10.55   Head of Fourth Year leaves. Deputy Head goes to the staffroom.

10.59   To the staffroom, then to Lower School building. Meets caretaker on the way. They talk in passing. Deputy Head's 'bleeper' goes off. He hurries to a Lower School office to telephone in to the main school office.

11.05   Lower School secretary tells him that a teacher would like him to check a window in a classroom that is being blown about by the high winds. Asks boy outside the secretary's room why he is waiting there.

11.06   Goes to check the window in the classroom.

11.08   Returns to his own office in the main building. He is 'bleeped' en route. He goes directly to the school office in response to the paging.

11.10   Talks briefly to the school secretary about some coaches. Returns to his own office. He meets the caretaker on his way.

11.13   Gives a form to the caretaker in his office. The caretaker leaves.

11.14   Telephones County Hall about bus timetables. There is a knock on the door whilst he is telephoning. It is the Second Caretaker. He is asked to wait outside. He continues with his telephone call.

11.25   End of the call to County Hall. He invites the Second Caretaker into his office. They discuss caretaking arrangements after the retirement of the First Caretaker and before a replacement has been made.

11.33   A teacher knocks on the door. He is asked to wait outside.

11.38   Ends conversation with Second Caretaker. Goes to the door to look for the teacher who knocked. He has gone.

Other activities on the same day:

1   Re-writing bus schedules for the pupils on the Link Vocational Courses.
2   Arranging a programme for a visit by the Educational Psychologist.
3   Sticking up a number of 'What to do in case of fire' notices in different parts of the building.
4   Talking to the Head of Fifth Year about the poor morale in the year group.

Senior team Document IV: Maureen's duties

Pupil standards – jointly with all senior staff
School functions
Physical environment
School Brochure
Newsletter
Transition to FE
Liaison with community
Schemes of work ⎫ jointly with curriculum Deputy
Curriculum review ⎭ Headteacher
External exams
INSET – internal
Staff resources
Printer resources
Admin Handbook
Staff Handbook
School calendar
Home–away diary
Option system
Supervision of supply, temporary, probationers and students
Section 11 staff
Staff development
Staff welfare
Anti-racism and equal opportunities
Special Needs

Senior team Document V: Maureen's morning

8.25 Chat to Head of Special Needs as they come into school.
8.28 Sort papers in her room.
8.29 Walk to Head's office.
8.30 Senior staff morning briefing.
8.50 Walk to staffroom talking to Head of Lower School.
8.51 In staffroom talk to each supply teacher and probationer.
9.00 Sort papers in her room.
9.05 Meeting with Head of English and Headteacher about the English examination results in Head's office. Maureen leads discussion to previously circulated agenda, comparing results with last year, other subjects, between individual members of staff and plans for this year. Head says virtually nothing.
10.00 Chat to Head after meeting.
10.03 Similar meeting Head of Modern Languages and Headteacher.
10.58 Chat to Head after meeting.
11.01 Similar meeting Head of CDT and Headteacher.
12.00 Discuss morning with Headteacher.
12.15 In own room for previously arranged meeting with probationer about LEA form that needs filling in.
12.47 Community leader visits to discuss Urdu translation of the school brochure.
 1.05 Teach.

Senior team Document VI: Heads and Deputies; a point of view

Headteachers are clearly central figures in their schools, but this does not mean they should be dominant. Where all decisions, procedures, communications and systems are focused on the Head, serious weaknesses of management and organisation emerge.

Many Heads are frequently out of school because of the increased work needed outside on such things as negotiating with the LEA over staffing, resources and policy; visiting primary schools to recruit children; public relations visits with local organisations. Our research did not look at this work of Heads but it was apparent that many are out of school two days a week (a proportion also reported by Hall, Mackay and Morgan). It became obvious that significant management decision-making and implementation within the school needed to be undertaken independently by other members of staff as well as the Head, and without them feeling dependent on the Head for authorisation and confirmation of the decisions they made. Despite the need, this was rarely found in practice. Heads continue to find delegation very difficult and the burden of Headship is willingly *eased* by Deputies, but seldom *shared*.

We suggest that the two essential tasks for the Head are to be the mover of the mission and to manage the boundary. The first is a subtle, bridging activity involving, in Hoyle's words: 'identifying, conceptualising, transmitting and gaining acceptance of a mission for the school, an idea or image of where it is heading' (Hoyle, 1986, p. 123).

Leaders of this type have been variously described as *institutional* leaders by Selznick (1957), *transformative* leaders by Burns (1978), possessing *hands-on, value-driven* attributes by Peters and Waterman (1982), *poets* by Hodgkinson (1983) and *symbolic chief/high priests* by Sergiovanni (1984).

In moving the mission the Head makes use of the unique position that Headship confers of being the figurehead and principal representative of the school, the person to whom most information from the environment is first given, the recipient of the memoranda, the person in contact with the LEA, HMI and advisers, as well as being in touch with the school's clientele. That welter of data and ideas is then translated into plans:

> The Head who would create a mission for the school would have the continuous task of selecting from these clusters of knowledge

© Derek Torrington, Jane Weightman, Basil Blackwell Ltd, 1989.

which, as modified by an awareness of forces within the Head and within the teachers currently teaching in the school and such other organisational forces as structures and resources, would fashion a set of goals for the school which could be construed as a mission.

(Hoyle, op. cit., 1986, p. 125)

The nature of the mission is not likely to be brought down by the Head from a mountain top inscribed on tablets of stone, as it will involve extensive consultation to discover and clarify, but the Head will then *move* the mission by winning staff commitment to it and will move it further by actually making it happen. Splendid dreams and ideas that are excellent in principle are not as good as less grand schemes if it is only the latter that can be made to work. The Head can become the personal embodiment of the mission, by living out whatever it may be.

The second essential task of the Head is representing and selling the school in all the necessary dealings with the outside bodies on which the school depends, from the LEA 'office' to local employers, other local bodies, national educational institutions, courses and conferences and the local press. The risk in all of this is of becoming a showman, a rather stagey figure who loses touch with the school and loses the confidence of the staff.

The first task requires Heads to be out and about in the school; the second task requires Heads to be out of school a lot. Consequently, they cannot do the other management jobs; something has to be given up. It is not appropriate for a Headteacher to be involved in everything. For example, appointing junior staff could more sensibly be done by the Head of Department and some other senior staff member, such as the staff development teacher, but in every school we visited Heads in practice decided the appointment of *all teaching* staff.

Although Deputy Heads have the word 'deputy' in their title, this can be no more than an incidental part of their role. To have value they must be in charge of something important. If they were called, for example, Curriculum Manager or Personnel Manager this would be describing a coherent job and not just bits of the Headteacher's job. A Deputy Prime Minister is seldom a person of great influence unless that function is added to a 'real' job, like Home Secretary or Chancellor of the Exchequer. By giving each Deputy a proper job to organise and develop, a senior team of self-confident, competent professionals comes into existence that can enrich the life of the school, provide an efficient and valued service to the staff and make the job of

Deputy Head a job to relish rather than to die in. Deputies then take on the essential, discrete tasks of implementation that fall outside the responsibilities of Heads of Department, Heads of Year and similar office holders. This seems to us a more productive use of experienced, senior staff than their most frequent role at present, which is to be the butt of dissatisfaction within the school.

These comments should not be construed as grumbling about megalomaniac Heads. It is not a simple suggestion that Heads should relinquish some of their power, it is equally a plea that Deputies should be much more assertive and creative in their approach to their jobs. Many of the Deputies who complain of being denied *authority* by their Heads are quite pussy-footed about accepting the *responsibility* that is the necessary concomitant of the authority they seek.

There is essential work to be done by both the Head and Deputies, but this work needs to be shared so that each person has areas of responsibility to take decisions about, influence others and make things happen. This sharing not only helps the school to run well, it also enables other staff to develop their contribution, their careers and themselves. Even if they disagree with the Headteacher's view on an issue, when work is shared they do not run the risk of undermining the Headteacher's position.

Senior team Document VII: The effective Head

This is an example of how one Head, Daniel, empowered the Deputy Heads. It is a different approach from that of Peter Ford, in a different situation.

Daniel spent most of his time liaising with the LEA and local college and trying to increase the resources for the school. He also prepared well-argued, written papers for his governors. He left the day-to-day running of the school to the senior staff. As he said: 'My intention is to produce policy statements but not the doing. Some are local to the school, others are from the LEA. I also list priorities for the next twelve months and if they are not done we have failed'.

In conversation he frequently said 'I expect senior staff to deal with that'. For example, the examination results were reviewed in interviews between the head of department and one of the Deputy Headteachers. Staff development interviews with probationers were held by one of the Deputy Headteachers.

The effectiveness of Daniel's delegation was seen by the frequency with which other senior staff were going to meetings or bringing information in. If we compare him with Peter Ford we find several differences.

1 The traditional *position* of Headteachers. Clearly, this applied to all Headteachers to some extent but Daniel worked in a local authority which was more centralised than Peter Ford's, so he needed to spend a great deal of time liaising with the LEA officers over policy, nuances of interpretation in official statements and detailed arrangements about resource provision.

2 *Historical* factors. Daniel's school had a very high profile in the 1970s and 1980s. It was seen as progressive and innovative. During the early 1980s it had a high profile Headteacher who had made lots of changes in his three year stay and then moved on. Daniel had worked in the school for 15 years and was appointed Head after being Acting Head for a year. He was trusted by long-established staff as having the interests of the school at heart, and he was expected to stay. Many felt the school could do with settling down.

3 *Individual loyalty.* Many of the staff who had worked with the Head before his promotion shared many of his values. Staff felt free to develop interests and ideas without so much constraint as previously. Some junior staff felt they did not know the Head-

© Derek Torrington, Jane Weightman, Basil Blackwell Ltd, 1989.

teacher but took their queries, and developed their loyalty, to heads of department/year or other colleagues in the staffroom.

4 *Information*. Daniel kept up-to-date on LEA policy and issues. Other members of staff were seen as the sources of information about the community, new initiatives and ideas. There were formal meetings where this information could be exchanged, for example, daily senior staff briefings. Informally, a great deal was exchanged in the staffroom and when coffee was provided at break time.

5 *Senior Management Group*. Five of the six senior staff, besides the Head, had clear roles. These were, Head of Curriculum, Head of Administration and Staff, Head of Upper School, Head of Lower School and TVEI Co-ordinator. The sixth was a helpful member of staff who filled in for the others but lacked any clear role and, consequently, lacked credibility with the staff. Daniel did not interfere with the work of the senior staff, they were free to take decisions, convene meetings and get things going without him.

13 Change
Ray Sylvester

We now pick up part of the theme of valuing introduced in chapter 5 and develop it in relation to improving the climate for change in a school. The materials include notes for a number of different scenarios from school life, which can be used either for group discussion or for role-playing. Group size could be up to 20 people.

On completion members of the group should be able to:

a) understand a range of problems that inhibit change in schools;
b) develop responses to those problems;
c) make possible teacher commitment to change.

Participants will need:
Change Document I – *Facing differences*
Change Document II – *Facing people*

To the trainer

There is no shortage of advice, in books and journals concerned with the management of schools, regarding the formal organisational structures which might be set up to create an adaptive environment conducive to change. There is clear evidence that some structures are better at adapting to a changing environment than others: that systems which involve staff through some form of consultation, or even participation, in decision making are better than those based on bureaucracy or autocracy. The Holy Grail for so many curriculum innovators is to find the right balance between stagnation and innovation-overload and ensure that the changes which are envisaged are 'owned' by the staff, even if these changes originate elsewhere (the Government, LEA or Headteacher's priorities, for example). It is recognised that this objective will not be achieved and that teachers' scepticism, fears, and at times hostility towards change, will not be minimised unless there is a change in the prevailing climate of the school. In practice this means paying attention to people and relationships as well as structures and organisation; concentrating on the nature and quality of the adult relationships within the school as well as the achievement of particular goals or tasks. Writers such as Murgatroyd (1984) maintain that the primary task of senior management within a school is to:

> permit, enable and encourage the development of relationships which make the achievement of tasks possible ... (and to) ... engage in self-disclosure themselves and show empathy, warmth, respect and support for others who do likewise ... and encourage self-awareness.
>
> (p. 173)

Another writer (Kanter, 1985) talks about the need to encourage teachers to question change and argues that discussion should be promoted, confrontation and criticism regarded as constructive, more open communications encouraged and information shared on a face-to-face basis. All well and good in theory, but how do you go about creating such a climate, assuming that its achievement is thought desirable?

The first step to improving the climate is for teachers at all levels to be aware that whenever we interact with our colleagues, in informal as well as formal situations, there can be positive or negative results in terms of the effect on the climate of the school. This is particularly true when considering the work of senior management, when the need to act quickly often undermines the longer term need to improve the quality of the adult relationships in the school.

This exercise attempts to raise the level of awareness of these situations by presenting a number of management 'problems' and a range of alternative responses to those problems. Participants are asked to consider which alternative, or combination of alternatives, would be *more likely*, over a period of time, to create a more open, trusting and warm climate – a climate more conducive to change. This may not be the most 'efficient' response; and it will certainly take more time and involve direct interaction with colleagues, but it will have a beneficial long term effect on the climate of the school, raising levels of morale and teacher commitment.

It is hoped that the scenarios, all of which have been drawn from or based on situations witnessed by or described to the writer during his work with the 'MOSS' Project, have the 'ring of truth' about them, even if they do not describe the particular reality in the reader's own school. The scenarios are set in the context of the work of senior management, although it goes without saying that the climate of a school will only improve if everybody accepts their share of the responsibility for improving it. Having said that, it could be argued that senior management does have the main responsibility for helping to ensure that the 'climate is right'!

These scenarios could be used in a number of ways in a training context:

1 Groups of teachers could be instructed not to look at the 'solutions' but concentrate on the 'problems'. They should describe their own solutions, individually and then in groups, and only then refer to the alternatives listed. Teachers will, no doubt, come up with many answers that are not listed and many that are. The main criterion to be used in assessing the 'answers' is: which would do most to improve the climate of the school? Which of the listed answers would have a similar effect?

2 Individuals could select their preferred solutions from the alternatives listed and then compare their decisions with those of colleagues in their group.

3 Selected scenarios could be used as a basis for a role-play exercise. Individuals could be given the role of the senior manager and asked to react to colleagues who have been briefed to behave in accordance with the scenarios. The listed solutions could be used as a basis for discussion during the debriefings which would follow the role play.

The way that the Headteachers *actually* responded to these scenarios is shown at the end of the chapter.

The scenarios have been built around two organising concepts – *facing differences* and *facing people*.

Document I: *Facing differences* is based on the notion that if senior staff want to increase levels of trust and openness they must recognise the plurality of interests within their community. The value differences between teachers must be faced and some way found of living with them. In a phrase made popular by Holly (1986), schools should not conspire to put *'deep-seated value conflicts to bed ... (where) ... they are allowed to remain dormant'*. Differences over values must be allowed to surface, even if this means upsetting the dream or myth of cultural cohesion.

Document II: *Facing people* is predicated on the very simple notion that teachers need to be valued and appreciated and that senior management should find time to do this by talking to people whenever possible. Although a written memo might suffice in a particular situation it may be more advantageous in terms of improving the climate of the school if that same message were transmitted directly, on a face-to-face basis.

References

Murgatroyd, S, 'Relationship, change and the school', *School Organisation*, Volume 4, Number 2, 1984.
Kanter, RM, *The Change Masters*, London, Unwin, 1985.

Change Document I: Facing differences

1 *The Head of Upper School has requested a change in the traditional timing of the mock exams. The Headteacher is not in favour of this change.*

Should he:

- Place the subject high on the agenda of the next HoD meeting, knowing that the majority of the HoDs may agree with the HUS?
- Refuse the request outright?
- Consult individual HoDs in his office, making his viewpoint quite clear?
- Agree to the HUS's proposal whilst at the same time distancing himself from it?

2 *The new Headteacher is not in favour of your school's very formal Prizegiving. The style of the occasion does not accord with her philosophy.*

Should she:

- Consult the staff, making her philosophy plain and asking for suggestions for revitalising the proceedings?
- Announce that she has decided to completely abandon the occasion?
- Allow the occasion to go ahead for that year whilst planning to review the situation for the future?
- Announce her disapproval of the current format and present her improved version to the staff as a fait accompli?

3 *During a staff meeting an issue is raised which the senior manager chairing the meeting considers could be controversial and possibly divisive.*

Should the chairperson:

- Refer to the agenda and point out that there is no time to discuss this matter?
- Allow the issue to be aired for a short time and then close down discussion?
- Give the discussion free rein whilst observing formal procedures?
- Allow a short discussion and then arrange to consider the matter in a more appropriate context?

© Derek Torrington, Jane Weightman, Basil Blackwell Ltd, 1989.

4 *The Senior Management Team wishes to establish a number of cross-curricular TVEI (E) groups within Directed Time. Staff are expected to opt into one or another of the groups. There are a number of staff who show no inclination to do so.*

Should the Senior Management Team:

- Do nothing and hope that the involvement of the rest of the staff will shame them into action?
- Announce to the staff that those who have failed to opt in will be allocated places in appropriate groups?
- Identify the staff concerned and make the opportunity to have a quiet word with each one and try to enlist their cooperation?
- Direct the 'dissidents' to meet a member of the team, whilst their colleagues are engaged in their TVEI (E) group activities, for some form of collective counselling?

Change Document II: Facing people

1 *The Head of Maths reports to a member of the senior management team that one of the teachers in the department is having problems.*

Should the manager concerned:

- Tell the HoD, in effect, 'It's your problem. You solve it!'?
- Offer help whilst reminding the HoD that ideally it should be solved within the department?
- Send a formal memo to the teacher in question with an appointment for an interview?
- Contrive an informal chat with the teacher in question, on neutral territory, with a view to establishing a relationship wherein the teacher might be more prepared to discuss their difficulties?

2 *The Headteacher has a weighty problem on her mind. She passes a junior member of staff in the corridor who gives her a breezy 'Good morning.'*

Should the Headteacher:

- Respond in kind?
- Ignore the greeting totally?
- Stop for a brief chat asking how the teacher is progressing?
- Stop and share her problem with the teacher?

3 *A letter has been received from the LEA about your school which causes the Headteacher a good deal of concern.*

Should he:

- Retreat into his room in an attempt to solve the problem himself?
- Call an emergency staff meeting bringing the matter out into the open and asking for staff reactions?
- Share the problem with his Senior Management Team and Chairman of the Governors in confidence?
- Discuss the matter informally with as many staff as possible?

4 *A Deputy Head witnesses a confrontation between a teacher and a child which she feels the teacher is handling badly.*

Should the Deputy Head:

- Intervene in the confrontation?
- Walk past and, when she can do so, ask the teacher's Head of Department to see the teacher concerned about the way the child was managed?
- Find an opportunity to talk to the teacher concerned, pointing out that there might have been a better way of handling the situation?
- Discipline the child herself, and inform the Head of Year but not talk to the teacher?

5 *You and your colleagues have pulled out all the stops to make an Open Day a resounding success.*

Should the Headteacher:

- Comment on individual classroom displays etc when he meets the teachers responsible?
- Offer a blanket 'Thank you' the next time he sees the staff as a whole?
- Formally thank the HODs and ask them to pass on his thanks?
- Write a note thanking the staff which he pins on the staffroom noticeboard?

6 *The calendar for the Summer Term is being planned when it is realised that the proposed date for the School Concert is no longer convenient. A decision has to be made quickly.*

Should the teacher responsible for planning the calendar:

- Find the Head of Expressive Arts to discuss a possible change of date?
- Write a memo to the Head of Expressive Arts requesting an interview?
- Change the date and then inform the Head of Expressive Arts?
- Change the date and put the revised calendar on the staffroom noticeboard?

7 *The new Headteacher has inherited a number of Heads of Department who are resistant to change, particularly with regard to the view they have of their management roles. The Headteacher wants them to change their attitudes.*

Should she:

- Have a pleasant chat with them in her office with a view to bringing them round to her way of thinking?
- Do nothing and wait until they can be replaced with new appointees?
- Direct them to attend off-site courses or arrange for a management consultant to come into school to train them in modern management techniques?
- Identify and nurture subordinates within the departments who will ferment change from below?

8 *The National Curriculum has marginalised Mr Peabody's special subject but the timetable offers him the 'opportunity' to teach in other areas. He is reluctant to diversify.*

Should the Deputy Head (Curriculum):

- Ignore his protests and write him into the new timetable where it is convenient?
- Point him in the direction of the LEA's early retirement scheme?
- Provide the opportunity for some form of counselling where he could express his anxieties and hopefully come to terms with the need for change?
- Have a friendly chat with him in an effort to change his mind?

9 *A teacher presents the Deputy Head (Curriculum) with an idea for developing an aspect of the curriculum. The DH is not altogether convinced that the idea is a good one.*

Should the DH:

- Briefly explain that the idea has been unsuccessfully tried elsewhere and refuse permission?
- Refer the teacher back to the HoD knowing that the HoD is not keen on the idea?
- Inform the HoD that you intend to give the teacher permission to implement the idea and ask for constant monitoring?

© Derek Torrington, Jane Weightman, Basil Blackwell Ltd, 1989.

- Discuss the idea at length making sure the teacher has considered all the implications before giving conditional permission?

10 *County Hall wants a report on a probationary teacher. The Headteacher realises that she knows very little about the teacher concerned.*

Should she:

- Send the letter to the Deputy Head responsible for staffing?
- Visit the probationer's classroom, with or without warning, and view a lesson?
- Invite the probationary teacher to her room for a chat?
- Find an opportunity to sit next to the probationary teacher at lunch, in the staffroom or around the school and make informal enquiries?

11 *A copy of an anthology of children's verse, produced by a teacher in the English Department, has been placed in the Headteacher's in-tray.*

Should the Headteacher:

- Send a note to the teacher concerned commending him on his efforts?
- Make a mental note to mention the production of the anthology in any future reference he writes on the teacher?
- Make a point of seeing the teacher personally and congratulating him on a job well done?
- Ask the Head of English to pass on his thanks to the teacher concerned?

Section Three
WHOLE SCHOOL REVIEWS – MANAGERIAL AND ADMINISTRATIVE INITIATIVES

The final section of the book deals with possible managerial and administrative initiatives that could be taken in relation to the whole school. The assumption is again of people working in groups. The exercises are:

14 Organisation charts: how the line management and hierarchy affect the organisation
    Group discussion on methods of management improvement
15 Geography and staffrooms: their role in effective organisation
    Group discussion on improving effectiveness through improving facilities
16 Managing the timetable: participation in decision-making and distribution of resources
    Group discussion on methods of management improvement
17 Communications II: why meetings are held
    Group discussion on how to improve meetings
18 Finance: keeping the books
    Group discussion on methods of management improvement
19 Core and periphery staff: their different needs
    Group discussion to introduce a new concept
20 Communications III: the briefing meeting
    Group discussion on how to introduce briefings
21 The poor performer: the hardest problem to tackle
    Group discussion on methods of management improvement

14 Organisation charts: how the line management and hierarchy affect the organisation

The structure of the organisation is usually taken for granted, but an inappropriate structure can seriously weaken organisational efficiency. These notes are for a small group (3–4) of senior staff to consider ways of re-organising the school with the implications of such re-organisation.

On completion participants will be able to:

a) see consequences of various formal arrangements;
b) develop worked-out ideas for change.

Participants will need:
Charts Document I – *Organisation charts*
Charts Document II – *Job titles*
Charts Document III – *Indicators of status*

To the tutor

All secondary schools have to divide up for day-to-day working to give each person a manageable chunk of work. So there are subject specialists, pupil specialists, whole-school policy specialists. This segmentation is essential; it breaks down the large number of people into smaller groups where informal contact is easier. This segmentation is described formally in such devices as organisation charts and job descriptions. In bureaucratic structures, which teachers' pay structures encourage, there is a formal hierarchy with implicit, if not always explicit, line managers. Clearly, these formal structures are overlain with the informal arrangements with which we all work. Indeed, many formal structures on organisation charts are historical. Close examination of any school's job titles and allocation of promotions tells one as much about their history as the current situation. However, some formal segmentation is required unless the whole school staff is prepared to invest considerable time in constantly re-negotiating who works with whom on what.

Organisation charts

1 Distribute Document I and discuss what type of structure each school has.

   Francis Bacon shows a faculty structure with clear line managers and Head of Faculty. The senior teachers, responsible for the pastoral side, are divided into years.

   William Barnes shows a department structure with Heads of Department. The pastoral side is organised into Houses with two Heads of Houses as the line managers.

   Hall End attempts to give line management position to people with both a subject and a pastoral responsibility.

2 Discuss areas where there might be frustrations. For example:
   a) The obvious inequality between the sexes, except in **Hall End**.
   b) The dual roles of Head of Department/Head of House in **William Barnes**.
   c) The difference in status between Heads of Upper School and Lower School in **Hall End**.

Questions for discussion:
- Can you find examples of historical positions?
- What co-ordinating devices would you need in each of the schools?
- Where do you think the integrating comes from?
- Are there any individuals who seem overloaded?
- Are there any who seem isolated?

(No more than 20 minutes)

3 Distribute Document II and ask people to work in groups of three or four. *Tasks for them to undertake are:*
- How would you arrange these jobs into an organisation?
- What are the shortcomings of this chosen way?
- What sort of decision-making groups would you need?
- Does anyone have an overload?
- How could the organisation be made apparently more efficient by merging or abolishing jobs on this list?
- Should any jobs be added?

(About one hour)

4 Other questions you might like to raise are:
- Draw an organisation chart for your school based on one of the examples given. Can you find a place for each person? What about those with dual roles? What does this tell you about the complexity of the segmentation? What does it tell you about the need for co-ordinating devices? Who has jobs that appear to

integrate things? What about those who do jobs that are not listed on the formal staff list?

- What are the main line management responsibilities of the Heads of Department in your school? How do they vary in their interpretation of this? Is there anyone else in the school with a line management responsibility? What about non-teaching staff?

At least 30 minutes)

Differential indicators of status

Sites, sections and departments acquire status within a school. There are various indicators of this status.

Develop a discussion about what status indicators there are. Some are listed here, although not necessarily in the order of weighting that affects status.

a) The extra salary given to the department, site or section for responsibilities carried out within it.

b) The number of staff within the department.

c) The extent to which the subject is seen to have status within the curriculum core.

d) The quality of the rooms and equipment provided for the department.

e) The quality of the timetabling for the department and the number of non-contact periods allocated.

f) The number of part-timers or non-specialist staff who teach the subject.

g) The amount of capitation or other resources given to the department.

h) The presence of a senior member of staff within the department and the quality of that person, if he or she has been chosen to take on the role within the department.

i) The presence of the Head of Department on senior decision-making bodies within the school.

j) Adviser, county or national support for the department or what it is doing.

k) The aggressiveness or acquisitiveness of the Head of Department.

l) The quality of administration and management within the department and how this is perceived.

m) Success of the department's pupils in examinations or other public achievements.

n) The qualifications or the quality of experience of the staff teaching within the department and the amount of non-teaching support it has.

o) The order on the timetable or on department lists.

p) Area, county or national status of the department, often shown by visitors to the department from outside.

All these factors can contribute to the morale of the teachers within the department. Where a department has low status or a low self-image, it is important that efforts are made to change this.

Some schools, consciously or not, concentrate the more attractive resources on a few people, whereas other schools have a more equitable arrangement. The consequences of concentrating resources on a few is to support the hierarchy, increase a feeling of 'them and us', and isolate those with privilege from those without. The consequence of an equitable arrangement is that resource allocation no longer indicates status and the opportunity of rewarding special effort or difficult circumstances is lost. However the various indications of status are allocated, members of an organisation have a very refined understanding of minute changes.

(30 minutes)

2 Distribute Document III and ask members to work in mixed groups of three or four to discuss it. It is important to ensure that an answer to the last question is started.

(At least one and a half hours)

Charts Document I: Organisation charts

Here are three examples of schools who have chosen different types of formal structure. (This was under the old-style salary scales.)

HALL END

Scale	MATHS	HUMS	SCI.	ART	SPECIAL NEEDS	ENG.	PE	HOME EC	CDT	MOD LANG	ESL	Other	FDrama	FMusic
HT	M (Music)													
DHT	MHoUS (Maths)		FCurric. (Science)			FAdmin. (Eng.)								
ST		FHoLS (Hums)					MTVEIC (T)(Sci)	F(Soc. Study)						
4	M(HoD)	M(HoD)	M(HoD) (T)	F(HoD)	F(HoD) HoY1	M(HoD)	F(HoD) M(Project)	F(HoD) Ho4Y F(Project)	M(HoD)	F(HoD) (T)	F(HoD)	MCareers; MSoc. Sci. Ho3Y; FRE PSG (T); MACS Word.	FDrama	FMusic (PT)(T)
3			M M(T)				MHo5Y (T)	F	M	F(HoD)	FF			
2	M F(Project)	MHo2Y FHoD Geog.		F(T)	F(Project)	M	F	F	M	F(T)	FF		F(T)	
1	M		FF FG	M	FF	F F	F	F	M F					

PT = Part time
T = Temporary
Vacancy Scale 3 HoD Music

WILLIAM SHAKESPEARE

		HT	DHT	ST
		M(Econ)	MA Admin (Sci)	FA 6th Form (Art)
			MB Pastoral (5 subjects)	MB Options (Chem)
			MC Curriculum (4 subjects)	NC P Liaison (Maths)

	MSci	Maths	Eng	Geog HoH(1) M	Hist HoH(1) M	RE HoH(2) M	ML HoH(3) F	Music M	Careers F / Assessment & Profile M(Eng)	Bus. Studies F	CDT M HoH(1) M	Spec. Needs M	Home Econ F	Art M	PE B M / G F
4		M	M	M	M	M	F	M	F	F	M	M	F	M	B M / G F
3	Chem HoH(4) F / Physics M	Comput. M M	Socio/ Eng M	HoH F(2) HoH M(3)	F		German F	M			M	F	FF	MM	M
2	Bio M	MMF	S/E Lib F F F		M	F	M	M		M	M	F	FF	MM	M
1	F M F(PT)	M F(PT)	M F(PT)	F(PT)	M		F			M	M	4 Home Tutors			M

A ⎫
B ⎬ Buildings in the school.
C ⎭

HoH = Heads of House 2 per house.

FRANCIS BACON

Headteacher M

Deputy Heads M M F

	CREATIVE STUDIES	HUMANITIES	MATHS & SCIENCE	LANGS	Special Learning Services	Hearing Impaired Unit
		Head of Faculty M / Head of English F	Head of Faculty M / Head of Maths Sc 4 F			
Sc 4	M				M	
Sc 3	M M F	M M M	M M F	M		F
Sc 2	M F	F F F F	M M M F F F F F	F F		
Sc 1	M M M F F F F F F F	M M F F F F F F	M M M M M F F F F F F F	F F F F	M F F	F F F

30% of this staff
are females on scale one

PUPIL SUPPORT TEAM

Senior Teacher   Hd. Lower Sch. M   Hd. of Sixth Form M

Year Co-ordinators – Sc 4   Yr1 F   Yr3 M   Yr4 M   Yr5 M

Charts Document II: List of job titles from a school

Scale	Job title
T2	Integrated Curriculum/English
4	Head of Lower School/Head of Integrated Curriculum
2	English/Library
2	Section 11
H	Head
3 T4 (ACS)	Head of Art
3	On exchange (Head of Languages)
3	Head of Drama
2 T4	Head of Science 1986/87
/	Languages
2	Science/Control Technology
1	Home Economics
2	Physical Education/Outdoor Pursuits
1	Art
2	Integrated Curriculum/Primary Liaison
/	Research Associate/Centre for Research in Ethnic Relations (CRER)
2	Integrated Curriculum
I3	Head of Music
4	Head of English/Acting Head of Languages 1986/87
1	Integrated Curriculum/English
2 T3 (ACS)	Maths/Computers
3	Business Studies
ST	Head of Upper School/Humanities
4	On secondment (Head of Science)
2	Special Needs
4	Section 11
1	Languages
2 T3 (ACS)	ACS Co-ordinator
T2	Integrated Curriculum/Humanities
1	Physical Education
2	Science
4	Co-ordinator for Special Needs
3	Head of CDT
3	Head of Home Economics
4	Head of Mathematics
2	Maths

DH	Deputy Head/English
1 Supply	Special Needs (Part-time)
4	Head of Humanities
T2	Integrated Curriculum
1	ACS/Art/Humanities
3	Maths
1	Science
DH	Deputy Head/English
2	Section 11
DH	Deputy Head/Science
ST	Head of Middle School

Youth Tutor (On secondment 1986/87)
Youth Club Leader

Registrar
Clerical Assistant
Non-Teaching Assistant
Technician
Senior Lab Technician
Lab Technician
Technician
Caretaker

T=Temporary 1986/87

Charts Document III: Indicators of status

Departments or Faculties

Salary									
Staffing									
Timetable									
Rooms									
Non-Specialist Teachers									
Capitation									
Senior decisions									
Public achievements									
Others									

1 Grade each department for each of the items listed, plus any others pertinent to your school.
   Score 1 for above average
         2 for average
         3 for below average
2 Which departments are best off?
3 Which are worst off?
4 How does this affect the school?
5 How does this affect individuals?
6 What are the worst problems?
7 What can be done about them?

15 Geography and staffrooms: their role in effective organisation

The last chapter examined the hierarchy of working relationships, this chapter considers the physical distribution of the people who have those working relationships. There are a series of topics for discussion and a short questionnaire about the staffroom. The exercise is suitable for staff at any level in the school, but ideally the work should be done by a group who have some chance of being able to introduce changes.

On completion participants should be able to:

a) Find ways of improving the use of their buildings;
b) Appreciate the importance of the staffroom.

Participants will need:
Geography Document I – *The location of kettles*
Geography Document II – *Staffroom questionnaire*

To the trainer

This set of materials deals with aspects of the school that are mostly suffered in silence or not even considered: the location of staff 'centres' and the way the staffroom is used. There are notes for an introductory talk and then some points for discussion.

Introductory talk and discussion

Geography and housekeeping are significant hygiene factors. When not properly dealt with they can cause major problems: when put right, they will not, of themselves, make working relationships perfect.

Buildings

Teachers, like everyone in employment, frequently mention that communications are poor in their school because of the building. Sometimes this is just an excuse where other solutions to the problem are possible, sometimes the communications are adequate anyway but undoubtedly it is easier to maintain relations in some buildings than in others.

Get the group to brainstorm the advantages and disadvantages of different sorts of buildings. Many disadvantages will quickly be suggested; advantages will be harder to identify. Some suggestions are given below.

Type of building	Effect on relationships	
	Advantages	**Disadvantages**
Split site	Smaller units so each able to be more cohesive	Difficult to have whole school feel
	More autonomy for each, so easier to feel participation in new ideas	Rapid distribution of information difficult
		Breaks spent travelling
Elongated	Almost a variation of split site	
Quadrangles	See each other across the quad frequently	Additions tend to be out on a limb and very isolated
	Sense of whole school	
Temporary classrooms (hutted settlement)	Autonomy	Difficult communication
	Flexible use of space for timetabling	Problems with centralised resourcing

(About 30 minutes)

Locations within the building

Layout within the building also affects relations and is more easily changed by those working in the school. The obvious issues are whether all senior staff should have offices together or dispersed, which room should be used as the staffroom and where the non-teaching staff are located. In most schools departments are grouped together geographically and this is felt to enhance relationships within departments. Often there is a departmental cubbyhole with kettle, where staff meet at breaks. Departments who are not located together often feel very aggrieved. Get members to briefly describe different ways of organising the location of:

- Senior staff offices – eg centralised/dispersed
- The staffroom – eg central/one end/several
- Non-teaching staff – eg together/dispersed
- Department rooms – eg in faculties/in years
- Pastoral staff – eg each with a room/all together

Point for discussion:
What are the advantages and disadvantages of each?

The importance of informal structures

Distribute Document I and discuss examples of informal arrangements that affect the members' schools.

This title is chosen to indicate the informal structures that develop within schools. These informal networks of contacts are an essential part of the running of any organisation as well as being an inevitable part of human groupings. The informal structures are communication networks, political alliances, mutually supportive groups, resource exchanges – in other words, people who come together because they choose to, not because they are supposed to. Most often these informal gatherings meet round coffee or tea – hence the title.

One Headteacher said to us: 'When I took over the school I banished all private kettles. They were only allowed to brew up in the staffroom.'

Points for discussion:
- After reading the document would you agree with this Headteacher?
- If you would agree, what would be the advantages and disadvantages of the decision in your own school?
- If not, what would your policy be and what would be the advantages and disadvantages of that policy?

(About 30 minutes)

The use of the staffroom

One aspect of teaching staff puritanism is where they tolerate poor facilities for themselves. Staffrooms are typically too small, poorly furnished, untidy, badly laid out and with coffee-making facilities that would disgrace a doss house. The staffroom is the hub of the school community, where information is traded, working relationships forged and innovation generated, as well as drooping spirits being revived, books marked, letters written and the host of everyday tasks of teaching back-up completed.

The quality of relationships in schools seems to be depressed where there are no good reasons for staff to use the staffroom. This is something easy to remedy and a matter of housekeeping.

1 Give out Document II and get members of the group to complete the short questionnaire.
2 Ask groups to discuss their findings.
3 Develop the discussion further, focusing on good reasons for staff to come to the staffroom. Some reasons are:
   • Good refreshments
   • Pigeonholes
   • Cover notices
   • Briefing meetings
   • Senior staff in?
   • What it looks like?
   • Telephone
   • Noticeboard
   • Timetable
   • Kept tidy

In schools where these factors exist, staff know they can find each other in the staffroom at particular times so can exchange information, fix dates, etc; new members of staff and periphery staff get to know people quicker; the school as a whole is more obvious. Perhaps most importantly, having reasonable staff facilities is not self-indulgence but rather an important part of ensuring the school works well.

This takes about 45 minutes.

Now continue the discussion by asking what other structures within schools encourage informal groupings and alliances. Ones we came across were:

• Sports, such as five-a-side football, netball.
• Particular issues such as feminism, shareholding syndicate.
• Shared interests such as theatre, recording studios.
• Swap shop such as gardening, children's clothing.
• Joint enterprise such as school trip, raising money.
• Shared experience such as TVEI weekend away, camp.
• Shared duties such as break, bus.
• Projects such as performance of play/concert, mural, farm.

British secondary schools cope with the whole gamut of interests and allow them to flourish. Much is lost by squashing them with over-neat, centralised, control systems, not only because of the value of the interests themselves, but also because they help sustain the organisation and provide a variety of opportunities for cross-school, informal contacts that people really value.

These informal contacts play a vital role in ensuring that the best possible job is being done by people working in the school. If people can choose the colleagues with whom they mix, they can develop trust; examine their own performance and what is sustaining or hampering that and decide what changes are appropriate.

As Ferguson (1980) says, writing about networks, 'Experience and insights are shared, argued, tested, adapted and shaken down into their usable elements very quickly' (p. 66).

Burns and Stalker, as early as 1961, described successful firms as having *organic* forms of organisation. Peters and Waterman (1982) have emphasised how successful organisations encourage the development of informal, flexible relations with a minimum emphasis on the formal hierarchy. Schools have always been good at this. It would be a serious error if the pressure to be more effective is distorted to an efficiency model that precludes the structures that sustain informal contacts within the school.

This takes about 20 minutes.

References

Burns, R and Stalker GM, *The Management of Innovation*, Tavistock, 1961.

Ferguson, M, *The Acquarian Conspiracy*, Granada, 1980.

Peters, T and Waterman, R, *In Search of Excellence*, Harper & Row, 1982.

Geography Document I: The location of kettles

The number and location of kettles in a school is a main determinant of the informal structure.

Usually there is at least a kettle – and sometimes more elaborate water boiling equipment – in the staffroom. There is also a kettle in the general office which supplies the Headteacher and some or all of the Deputies and senior teachers. This is a valuable clue to status in the informal structure: who within the senior staff is part of the inner coffee cabinet?

In addition to staffroom and general office facilities, there are at least the following informal structures based on the location of kettles.

Individual members of staff with kettles in their classrooms.

Some staff have kettles in their classroom or office and offer folk coffee/tea at break or when meeting someone. Mostly these are Heads of Department, in charge of subjects, or Heads of House.

Advantages of this approach:

- Each person develops their own network of contacts.
- Private conversation is possible with minimum interruption.
- Some very close-knit small groups develop.

Disadvantages of this approach:

- Suspicion that some people are being excluded.
- Difficulty of joining in if not specifically invited.
- Little casual involvement or incidental participation.

Departmental offices and prep. rooms where members of the department work in non-contact periods, meet to discuss things, keep the stock and make coffee.

Advantages of this approach:

- Lots of information, training and spontaneous, informal development of ideas.
- Team develops through mutual support for the development of individuals.
- Very supportive for new staff.

Disadvantages of this approach:

- The department can become so cosy that it is difficult to get involved with people in other parts of the school.
- Where a particular individual does not fit in with the rest of the team this problem is exacerbated.

- Cliquishness.

Geographically spread coffee bases where those who are working near each other take coffee together. At one school we found five sources of coffee: the staffroom, the dining room, Special Needs Department, the Science prep. room and the Art Department. Staff went to the coffee base nearest to where they happened to be working, which meant that each had some change of personnel day by day according to the variations of the daily timetable.

Advantages of the approach:

- The groupings were across departments so they heard about other people's concerns, initiatives, problems and successes.
- New people and supply teachers could easily join these groups as they were neither too intimidatingly large nor cliquey.

Disadvantages of this approach:

- Some departments may never meet informally because individuals are based near different kettles.
- It is difficult to know where to find a particular member of staff you are looking for.

Geography Document II: Staffroom questionnaire

Staffrooms

1 What proportion of the permanent staff enter the staffroom regularly (at least once a day)?

80%+ ....
60–79% ....
40–59% ....
25–39% ....
−25% ....

2 What are the three main staff activities in the staffroom? ....
....

3 Is the location of the staffroom convenient or inconvenient for general staff use? ....

4 Is the staffroom located in a pupil-intensive area or in an administrative area near to other offices, facilities etc? ....
....

5 Which non-teaching staff use the common room, and to what extent? ....
....

6 What form of coffee provision is there, if any? ....
....

7 Is smoking enough of a problem to discourage staff use of the room? ....

8 Are staff toilets convenient to the staffroom? ....

9 Which of the following are in, or adjacent to, the staffroom?
Phone.....................   Lockers.................
Noticeboard...........   BANDA................
Pigeonholes...........   Photocopier ....

10 Who, if anyone, takes care of the management of the staff-room?...
....
....

16 Managing the timetable: participation in decision-making and distribution of resources

This material aims to extend the understanding of those involved in timetabling issues about the wider implications of the timetable: it is not about the mechanics of the timetable. It is a practical exercise best undertaken by a group of three or four.

On completion participants should be able to:

a) understand the range of issues involved in compiling the timetable;
b) realise that the way timetable decisions are made is a clue to the management style of the school;
c) influence timetable decisions.

Participants will need:
Timetable Document I – *The process and the presentation*
Timetable Document II – *Requests received by timetable group*
Timetable Document III – *Distribution of non-contact time*

To the trainer

The person principally responsible for the timetable in most schools is either a Deputy Head or a senior teacher. Since the timetable is a critical co-ordination device, this makes sense – but only when that person is in a position to make decisions about the overall use of staff and physical resources. At one school, for example, the Deputy Head responsible for the timetable makes few major decisions about priorities, causing frustration and unnecessary delay. The Head then further delays a decision through instigating protracted discussion with other members of staff. The timetable in this school would be better drawn up by any numerate, flexible thinking member of staff. It does not require the efforts of this very conscientious, busy Deputy.

Help is occasionally (and sensibly) provided by a less senior member of staff for the more mechanical aspects of scheduling, such as testing the feasibility of option groups, rooming, or just plain copying out of details in alternative formats. Usually, however, it is a member of the senior staff who does these things. For some reason, this sort of unnecessarily tedious activity is unconsciously felt to be the justification for the Deputy Head's role. A greater investment by LEAs and schools in qualified administrative staff might resolve some of the problems of teaching staff spending their time carrying out such routine administrative tasks as translating the timetable into different formats.

The degree of consultation with other staff about curriculum issues affecting the timetable is varied. Two extremes we encountered were as follows:

At *Lodge School* the Head seemed to find great difficulty in devolving any responsibility to others, to the extent that she personally interviewed all sixth form candidates and drew up the options matrix on the basis of their responses. She also decided at this stage whether or not to run minority 'A' levels such as Latin, Religious Education and Music. She had only recently handed over the actual construction of the timetable to a senior teacher, and still exercised a great deal of non-negotiable control over its contents.

In contrast with this, *Jackson School* devolved the timetable to a sub-group of its Organisation and Administration Committee, with both open and pre-arranged representation. This group of about eight to 12 members of staff met regularly after school and was chaired by a Deputy Head. Matters in connection with the timetable were also discussed at Management Meetings and by the Curriculum Group, both of which met regularly and were, in theory, open to all staff. A member of the Geography Department (Scale 3), who had got interested in computerised timetabling via the Timetabling Group, put the timetable onto computer.

There are, of course, various advantages and disadvantages to both these styles. The staff at *Lodge* seemed to be quite content with the limited amount of say they had in curriculum and timetabling issues, but this arrangement had major implications for lack of ownership of what went on in the school. The extreme devolution found at *Jackson*, whilst achieving a remarkable degree of understanding of the timetabling process throughout the school, did, on the other hand, involve a great amount of repetitious discussion and hours freely given after school by a dedicated group of staff.

Those involved often fail to realise that consultation has to be a constant activity which occurs through good times and bad. Timetabling difficulties of other members of staff or other departments can often be resolved through peer group discussion. We discovered a few schools where it was left to Heads of Department to persuade their fellow HoDs to accept some timetabling change. We concluded that such mutual compromise, which did not depend on a single person to make a judgement about the validity of one case over the other, was an interesting variation in the decision-making process.

The process

The aim of this task is to bring to the attention of those responsible for the school timetable the wider process of planning, consultation and presentation. Although it is designed to be undertaken by the timetabler, it is also appropriate for any group of people who are involved with timetabling, or who are responsible for the curriculum.

This section is not concerned with the scheduling task which is known by some as 'timetabling'. The complex business of deciding when classes will be taught, where and by whom is already well documented and many timetablers do this aspect of the task very well already.

Hand out Document I and ask participants in groups of three to four to fill in the calendar.

This should take about 30 minutes.

Priorities

Introduce for discussion and development the issues of conflicts and priorities in timetabling; to consider valuing and weighting rather than the mechanics of implementation.

1 Divide participants into small groups of three or four.
2 Give each member of the group Document II for consideration.
3 Ask each group to discuss the requests and try to agree on an order of priority.
4 One member should record a summary of deliberations.
5 After roughly 20 minutes ask each group to finalise the top three priorities.
6 Reassemble as full group – and invite a member of each small group to report back on deliberations and conclusions.
7 Pick out main issues and highlight areas of consensus or disagreement.
8 Follow up in large/small group as appropriate with discussion of who should be involved in decision-making concerning timetabling priorities.

Non-contact time

There is a great deal of variation in the amount of non-contact time people have (see Figure 1). But non-contact time is seen as a privilege which needs managing.

Figure 1   Teaching loads of senior staff in six schools

School (Periods p.w.)		Head	Dep. Hd	ST	Ho Sch	HoF	HoD	HoY	HoH	School norm	School PTR
A	%	30	35	35–40	—	80	90	60–65	—	90	16.4
(40)	No.	12	14	14–16 (HoSch)	—	32	36	24–26	—	36	
B	%	4	32–52	48–56	32	—	68–80	68–80	—	80	14.2
(25)	No.	1	8–13	12–14	8	—	15–20	17–20	—	20	
C	%	0	32–36	40	—	—	64–68	—	—	72–84	8.8
(25)	No.	0	8–9	10 (HoSch)	—	—	16–17	—	—	18–21	
D	%	32	60	72–76	—	—	84	—	80	88	17.5
(25)	No.	8	15	18–19	—	—	21	—	20	22	
E	%	15	45–55	75–80	—	—	80–85	80	—	85	17.6
(40)	No.	6	18–22	30–32	—	—	32–34	32	—	34	
F	%	25	45–55	65–70	—	—	75	75	—	85	15.6
(40)	No.	10	18–22	26–28	—	—	30	30	—	34	

1 Distribute Document III and ask participants in small groups to fill it in. (This should take about 30 minutes.)

2 Discuss the findings, using the questions. (About 30 minutes.)

Timetable Document I – The process and the presentation

The task requires you to enter on the calendar provided the months in which you undertake the ancillary tasks listed below.

Tasks

Scheduling – assigning classes to teachers

Curriculum changes – consulting with appropriate staff on changes to the curriculum

Staffing – producing for a management group a staffing budget, with staffing availability matched with staffing needs

Heads of department requests – inviting heads of faculty/ department to make requests for specific blocking arrangements and for which staff are to teach which courses and classes

Rooms – inviting heads of department/faculty to assign teachers to rooms as best suits the needs of their department

Presentation meeting – calling a meeting of all interested staff to explain the new timetable and answer questions about it.

Print order – inviting staff to order full copies of the year, staff and room timetable in its different formats and sizes

Evaluation – circulating a timetable evaluation sheet to all staff to invite comments on the timetable they are operating

Review meeting – calling a meeting of all appropriate staff to consider the evaluation returns from teachers

Distribution and display – arranging for the distribution of timetables to staff, non-teaching staff and pupils. Displaying copies of the timetable in staffroom, school offices and pupil concourses.

Mailing – arranging for the mailing of timetables to all new members of staff

Options – meeting with teachers responsible for options programme to plan approaches to new timetable

Timetable team – choosing the teacher or teachers who will work with the timetabler as a member of the team

Now insert the tasks listed above in the table below: one item, scheduling, has been inserted as an example. You may feel that several of these tasks are not ones which are normally yours. In this event, fill in the name of the teacher or teachers who do the tasks. If the tasks are not carried out by anybody in your school, fill in at least one good reason why this is the case.

Date	Task	Undertaken by
September October November December January February March April May June July	 Scheduling	 Timetable team

Timetable Document II: Requests received by timetable group

'May I request, yet again this year, that for Fourth/Fifth Year English a morning or afternoon block is provided. Reasons as previously stated.'
M.A.S., Head of English Department

'Timetabled planning periods essential for discussion and curriculum planning for my department.'
A.H., Head of Humanities

'Must have Monday and Wednesday afternoons for 4th/5th Leisure Pursuits when sports centre is available to us.'
J.C., Head of Recreational Studies

'Please ensure that none of our classes are timetabled last thing on Friday. All morning periods if possible.'
T. S., Head of Maths

'Double periods are too long, as are single periods; twenty minute modules (as in Northland High) are ideal if conversational courses are to succeed.'
A.McL., Head of French

'1 Please ensure that no practical lessons are timetabled after assembly days.
 2 Adviser suggests we need more time for First/Second Year circus.
 3 Also DM/IB not to be used as tutors if possible (sharpening, etc.).'
D.M., Head of CDT

'Own classroom base essential if German is to develop as a second language.'
D.L.S., Teacher i/c German

'If I am to produce good results, Special Needs pupils from the third year groups should not be allowed to opt for Geography.'
Teacher i/c Geography

'One free period every day, preferably period one and not all on Thursday as this year.'
D.B., Head of Fourth Year

'Full blocking for 4th/5th Combined Sciences no longer possible as not enough equipment available at one time to meet the demands of the new practicals.'
R.F., Head of Science

Timetable Document III: Distribution of non-contact time

Consider the list given below and suggest an appropriate amount of non-contact time for the following positions.

Teacher	Out of 40 periods	Reasons for figure*
Headteacher A Deputy Head HoD Eng Sc 4 HoD CDT Sc 4 HoD Geo Sc 3 HoD PSE Sc 3 Exam Corresp. Sc 3 HoD Rec Stud Sc 3 HoY Yr 1 Sc 3 HoY Yr 5 Sc 3 i/c Drama Sc 2 i/c Wood Design Sc 2 Ass HoY Yr 4 Sc 1 Eng Sc 1 Maths (School Fund) Sc 1)		

*If unable to make a decision what other information do you need to know?

1 Make a personal list of two issues which have emerged as a result of undertaking this activity.
2 For which of the above teachers is the matter of non-contact time most problematical? Note down your reasons.
  (Group Activity) drawing together individual responses.
3 What is the average non-contact time for each of the above teachers?
4 Account for the main discrepancies between individual responses and the group mean.

17 Communications II: why meetings are held

These materials examine aspects of what might be called the micropolitics of meetings: the reasons for their being held and the problems of their ineffectiveness. The method is group discussion and a brainstorm.

On completing the exercise, participants should be able to:

a) Work out what meetings can achieve in schools and the problems caused by meetings which are not appropriate for their purpose;
b) Appreciate the overt and covert reasons for meetings being held;
c) Review the meetings held in their own school to find ways of improving their effectiveness through making sure that the process matches the content;
d) Work out alternatives to face-to-face meetings in some cases.

Participants will need:
Meetings Document I – *The Curriculum Planning Meeting*

To the trainer

This exercise is timed to take approximately two hours. It is appropriate for staff at all levels in the school and is best conducted in groups of between six and 12, although larger numbers are feasible. With careful organisation it could be used for a discussion among all staff, although there is the risk that one or two leading personalities could be embarrassed by what emerges.

The appendix on page 192 contains general notes about meetings which the trainer may wish to use in addition to the main exercise, which is set out below.

Introduction

1 Begin the session by reminding members of the group of the recent increase in emphasis on meetings in schools. When meetings are not possible, this is used as an excuse for lack of cohesion or progress;

where they *are* possible people complain of the time they take up but are nevertheless sure they are necessary.

2 Ask the group why meetings have become so important. Allow 15–20 minutes for this stage. Among the reasons to draw out from the discussion are:

- Teachers have a highly-structured, timetabled day. Timetabling meetings frees them from the classroom, shows that interaction with other adults is important and ensures that meetings are fixed in timetabled hours and not in preparation, marking and extra-curricular time.
- Meetings have become the focus of adult-to-adult interactions, being a legitimate part of a teacher's work, as well as the adult-to-pupil interactions.
- Face-to-face contact is emphasised in the classroom and consequently there is a desire for face-to-face contact in school management and organisation, rather than impersonal means.
- Education's liberal tradition, with its ideas of participative, consultative democracy, and the idea of a school as a community with an ethos of oneness, both make for a desire to get the tribe together.
- Many feel that properly run meetings could achieve the ideal of consensus, which many teachers hold dear, in contrast to the differences constantly shown up in the day-to-day life of school.

Now move the group on to consider the Curriculum Planning Meeting (Document I).

The Curriculum Planning Meeting

1 Distribute Document I and allow five minutes for everyone to read it.
2 Ask groups to suggest overt and covert reasons for the meeting, based on the notes. For example,

Overt reasons
a) *Making decisions* In the example they failed to decide about the school day but they did decide that the Special Needs Advisory Group Committee would meet regularly. Often pre-meeting discussions have made decisions and the formal meeting ratifies these.
b) *Making recommendations* The English teacher had thought about the study skills required by school leavers and the meeting recommended he and each of the heads of department discuss it separately.
c) *Training* – was not an overt reason although the Head of Special

Needs took the opportunity in his presentation to give details of the legal requirement the school has to meet these children's needs.

d) *Analysis and report* – would be when there was material to organise and another person or group to report to. The Deputy, making the presentation on INSET needs, has done this and in other circumstances the meeting might wish to prioritise the needs.

e) *Information* Giving and receiving information frequently takes place in meetings gathered for other reasons, most typically under matters arising and any other business, as in the example.

Covert reasons

a) *Cohesion* Physically bringing people together allows them to chat before/after, catch each other's eye, joke, feel part of the whole. In the example each subject department was represented and all felt part of the school.

b) *Catharsis* – allows people to get anger out even where nothing can be done about it. To some extent the Head of Science's frustration of the options achieved this.

c) *Manipulation* Often senior staff are accused of manipulation. Indeed, they frequently have discussed things before, so decisions have essentially been made prior to the meeting. In this example the Acting Headteacher could be accused of manipulating the agenda so that discussion about the school day was cut short.

d) *Involvement* The importance attached to participation is an obvious covert reason for holding meetings. The English teacher was given the opportunity to be involved in the meeting after his industrial visits.

e) *Learning* – about both content and process takes place but also the particular culture of this school and this meeting.

f) *Structures for dissent* Disagreement, conflict and dissent are an inevitable part of organisational life. Meetings can deal with this in different ways – by allowing heated discussion, suggesting that people report back next time or ignoring the dissent. All these happened in our example.

Members' experience of meetings

1 Ask members of the group to review different meetings they have attended and to identify which overt and covert purposes each meeting has served.
2 Ask them to think how other useful and relevant purposes could be served if the meetings were conducted differently.

3 Finally ask them to decide which meetings they would discontinue because they do not serve any useful purpose; ensure that their reasons are logical and that the meeting cannot be saved, or should not be saved.

Brainstorm: What are the alternatives?

Run a brainstorming session on how to achieve the best results from meetings by finding alternatives to attendance, or alternatives to the meetings themselves. Here are some ideas:

a) In what other way(s) can people be consulted, involved and part of making decisions?
b) How can meetings in schools be kept to a minimum number of people? By devolving a lot of decisions to departments? Increasing autonomy?
c) Currently a lot of paper is circulated in schools as preparation for meetings. Often the meeting just gives approval. Is there some way of signing and filing views to save time at meetings?
d) Where meetings are timetabled, do they always have to take place? Could other people put in a bid for this time and those timetabled cover for them? What about a system of bids for this slot?

Conclusion

Summarise the main points to emerge from the discussion throughout the session. Ask members of the group to identify specific changes in practice that they will try to introduce.

Appendix: General notes on school meetings

Meetings have become an important and time-consuming feature of school life, especially as the number of cross-school activities increases and the task of school management becomes more complex. Well-managed meetings can:

a) generate enthusiasm and focus involvement of staff in school affairs;
b) produce decisions to which a large number of people are firmly committed, thereby speeding the effective implementation of the decisions;
c) contribute to co-ordination and cohesiveness among staff members;

d) find fresh solutions to difficult problems;
e) provide means of communicating clear information quickly.

Among the many problems of meetings that are ill-conceived or poorly run are the risks of imagination and energy being expended to no avail, senior staff losing authority, problematic issues being aggravated through being exposed for public discussion without any resolution being found (the 'can of worms' problem), and the risk of consuming too much of that most precious school commodity – time.

The definition of a meeting

What is a meeting? For our research we did not tightly define what we meant by a meeting, as any definition produced anomalies, but we observed those occasions when people came together:

a) deliberately rather than accidentally (so we excluded casual conversations in the staffroom) ie planned in advance
b) to discuss official business relating to matters within the school
c) with usually more than two people present (so we excluded most one-to-one conversations)
d) to discuss matters outside the process of engaging directly with children in school (so we excluded school assemblies)

The research approach

Our observations included governors' meetings, full staff meetings, Heads of Department meetings, pastoral meetings, departmental meetings, working parties, curriculum development, staff development, senior staff, INSET, TVEI discussions, and so forth.

We observed and analysed 433 meetings, ranging from a few minutes to three hours in length. The greatest amount of time is always contributed by the most enthusiastic people, who are often the more senior members of the school, or those allowed space in their timetables. Meetings thus constitute a major investment of the time of skilled staff.

The management background

Although meetings probably consume much more managerial time in industry and commerce than in schools, the attention of management researchers has been patchy. Some aspects, such as team building and small group processes, are studied extensively; others, such as determining what types of meeting are needed, receive less attention. The evidence can be grouped under eight headings.

1 *Time spent* Two famous studies (Stewart, 1967 and Mintzberg, 1973) have included observation of the time spent in meetings. Stewart, studying 160 British managers, found that they spent an average of 34 per cent of their time in discussions with two or more people, of which 7 per cent was in committees. Mintzberg studied the work of five chief executives and found that they spent an average of 59 per cent of their time on scheduled meetings. The definitions thus differ slightly from our own but indicate the anticipated increase in the number of meetings for more senior people. This general tendency is apparent in schools, but the proportion of time spent in meetings is certainly lower for most, partly because of the timetables of those with whom they would like to meet. However, many senior staff in schools attend meetings in most lunchtimes and after school most days.

2 *Team work* There has been great interest, especially in recent years, in how management groups work as teams, using meetings as one of the ways of creating and sustaining the team. Drawing on the earlier work of Bales (1980) and Schein (1969), Eunice and Meredith Belbin (1981) studied the work of management teams and concluded that effective teams needed eight roles to be filled:

- *Company worker* – who keeps the organisation's interests to the fore
- *Shaper* – who influences by argument and by pursuing particular topics
- *Ideas person* – who contributes novel suggestions
- *Resource investigator* – who evaluates whether contributions are practical and finds out where and how to get the resources that are needed
- *Monitor/evaluator* – who assesses the validity of suggestions and the extent to which the team is meeting its objectives
- *Team worker* – who maintains the group process by agreeing, smiling and joking
- *Chairman* – who ensures all views are heard and keeps things moving
- *Completer/finisher* – who tries to get things done and suggests conclusions

Although we were unable to base our observation of meetings entirely on this model, these roles were clearly present in the meetings we observed, although (as elsewhere) one person would frequently fill several. Team workers and company workers are nearly always in another role as well and whoever was chairing the meeting often also acted as completer/finisher, monitor/evaluator, resource investigator and ideas person. Perhaps this occurs too often, so that the meeting is dominated by its leader, stifling initiatives from others and impairing the degree to which meetings can develop the confidence and participative efficiency of other members.

3 *Problem-solving* The use of meetings to solve problems produces a wider input of knowledge, information and varied approaches to the problem than problem-solving by individuals. The eventual solution will be owned by all, or most, members of the group and will therefore be better understood and more effectively implemented because of the broad basis of its ownership. Whilst generally producing better solutions than individuals, meetings do, of course, often mean that solutions take longer to be reached.

4 *Decision-making* Closely associated with problem-solving is decision making; and research usually studies the same processes. One difficulty with the group approach to problems is a tendency to snatch at the first acceptable possibility that is produced, with a strong preference for conservative solutions (Hoffman, 1979). Another difficulty is of certain group members beginning with a commitment to a particular solution so that the problem-solving process becomes a debate between two or more conflicting positions, with the advocacy tending to strengthen the varying commitments rather than open-mindedly seeking the best solution (Bazerman, *et al.*, 1984).

One unresolved question is that of the 'risky shift'. Groups will tend to opt for a riskier solution than will individuals faced with the same dilemma (Cartwright, 1971). Unfortunately there is not yet an explanation of what circumstances enable a group to be riskier than an individual.

5 *Conflict management* An inevitable by-product of the human organisation is conflict between its members. This is not always attributable to management error or organisational malaise. Although much conflict is dysfunctional, harming individuals and impeding the attainment of organisational goals, some is useful as it can be a force for creativity and innovation. Conflict finds its most fruitful expression in meetings, which are better than the alternatives of graffiti, anonymous letters, sabotage or nervous breakdowns. Meetings provide the opportunity for managers to manage the conflict rather than suggesting it, so as to minimise the damage it can cause and maximise the benefits it can confer (Rahim, 1985; Walton, 1969).

6 *Participation* Meetings provide one of the most popular vehicles for participation in the general running of the organisation by those who might otherwise make only a marginal contribution through their specialised duties. The machinery of collective bargaining in industry provides a range of consultation and the procedural structures that

accompany bargaining arrangements. These opportunities seem largely to be absent *within* schools although there may be considerable activity along these lines within the local authority.

Another development has been to use participation in the form of involvement, that is, not confrontational in the way that collective bargaining has to be. The best known recent examples are of *quality circles* (Bradley and Hill, 1983) which convene regular meetings of rank-and-file members of the organisation to discuss ways of improving quality, and *team briefing* (Thompson, 1983). The morning meetings of school staffs we observed were very similar to team briefing.

7 *Creativity* There has been some interest in the way group processes can stimulate innovation and unleash creativity in organisations. One set of techniques for this have been loosely grouped under the heading of *Organisation Development* (French and Bell, 1972). It is regarded as important that people are accepted by their work group, and if they are able to express their feelings about their group membership openly, rather than hiding their feelings, then they will be more innovative, confident and constructive. Another group technique is *brainstorming*, which is a method of generating a large number of different approaches to a problem or question (Rawlinson, 1981).

8 *Committees* Considering their prevalence, there has been surprisingly little study of committees, probably due to their formality which reduces the benefit which most researchers see resulting from informality. Committees are used to authorise action rather than work out what the action should be, and they are typically passive in deciding what they should do since matters are referred to them: seldom do they initiate their own business. An example in schools is often the Governors' meeting. There are many sources of advice for those who chair committees, although advice on how to be an effective committee member is less common (Torrington and Weightman, 1985).

Meetings in schools

We examined the following aspects of meetings in schools:

1 *Reasons for meetings* Meetings always had an overt, specific, declared purpose. This might be making decisions, formulating recommendations, or analysing a matter to make a report on the findings. Two other overt reasons were briefing and training. In addition to their declared purpose, the process of meetings served a number of other covert purposes: social cohesion of the staff, catharsis and the

expression of frustration, manipulation of individuals or groups to accept something they disliked, the general participation and involvement of staff members, learning.

2 *Types of meeting* We classified meetings into five types: meetings of the whole staff; secondly, those which were a 'vertical slice' of the staff with members from one particular area or speciality; thirdly, 'horizontal slice' meetings which drew members from across the organisation, like a meeting of Heads of Department; fourthly, those where people were involved mainly because of their expertise or interest in a general issue, like school discipline; and finally, there were the interface meetings, like case conferences, where the meeting included people from outside the school and dealt with matters which were not limited to the school.

3 *Meeting mechanics* We were able to identify various aspects of managing meetings that could improve their effectiveness: clarifying the right or duty to attend a meeting, the brief or terms of reference for a group holding a meeting, agenda, minutes, the report, chairing, being a group member, implementation of proposals, location and arrangements for meetings, the meetings calendar.

(2) and (3) above are dealt with in Part II of this book.

References

Bales, RF *Interaction Process Analysis*, Addison-Wesley, Reading, Massachusetts, 1950.

Bazerman, MH, Giuliano, T and Appleman, A 'Escalation of Commitment in Individual and Group Decision-Making', in *Organizational Behaviour and Human Performance*, Vol. 33, No. 2, 1984.

Belbin, RM, Aston, BR and Mottram, RD 'Building Effective Management Teams', in *Journal of General Management*, Vol. 2, pp. 23–9, 1976.

Bradley, K and Hill, S 'After Japan: The Quality Circle Transplant and Productive Efficiency', in *British Journal of Industrial Relations*, Vol. XXI, No. 3, 1983.

Cartwright, D 'Risk Taking by Individuals and Groups: An Assessment of Research Employing Choice Dilemmas', in *Journal of Personality and Social Psychology*, Vol. 20, No. 3, 1971.

French, WL and Bell, C *Organizational Development*, Prentice Hall International, Hemel Hempstead, 1973.

Hoffman, LR 'Applying Experimental Research in Group Problem-Solving to Organizations', in *Journal of Applied Behavioural Science*, Vol. 15, No. 3, 1979.

Mintzberg, H *The Nature of Managerial Work*. Harper and Row, London, 1973.

Rahim, A 'A Strategy for Managing Conflict in Complex Organizations', in *Human Relations*, Vol. 38, No. 1, 1985.

Rawlinson, JG *Creative Thinking and Brainstorming*, Gower Press, Aldershot, 1981.

Schein, EH *Process Consultation*, Addison-Wesley, Reading, Massachusetts, 1969.

Stewart, R *Managers and their Jobs*, Macmillan, London, 1967.

Thompson, F. 'The Seven Deadly Sins of Briefing Groups', in *Personnel Management*, February, 1983.

Torrington, DP and Weightman, JB *The Business of Management*, Prentice Hall International, Hemel Hempstead, 1985.

Walton, RE *Interpersonal Peacemaking*, Addison-Wesley, Reading, Massachusetts, 1969.

Meetings Document I

The Curriculum Planning Meeting

Every six weeks Summerfield High has a Curriculum Planning meeting attended by senior staff and Heads of Department. The agenda for this meeting was: Special Needs, Industrial Liaison, INSET the school day. It started at 3:40:

Acting Headteacher:	*Matters arising. Sorry, I forgot you're Chair.*
Acting Deputy Headteacher:	*Any matters? Anything?* (turning to Acting Headteacher)
Acting Headteacher:	*Update on options?*
Deputy Headteacher I:	*Just got options in. Finished tomorrow. Small number with difficulties in Science and Humanities.*
Acting Headteacher:	*Everyone clear what's happening – not sure?*
Deputy Headteacher:	*There are two groups of youngsters. Those who are graded 1–3 in Maths and English and the others. Top do English/Maths and six others. Lower do English/Maths/Integrated Humanities/ Integrated Science and three others, which may be GCSE or not.*
Head of Science:	*Low ability or eight periods of Science? Do top have to choose?*
Deputy Headteacher:	*We haven't put them off.*
Head of Science:	*But if Science is not compulsory a lot will give up.*
Acting Headteacher:	*Anything else?*

Discussion/complaint by Science Department over options and method of distribution of capitation to the Science Department.

3:53

Head of Special Needs gives detailed presentation about the need to look at Special Needs in departments and setting up a group with at least one person from each department.

Acting Deputy Headteacher:	*Is this group to meet regularly?*
Head of Special Needs:	*Yes, from Easter.*
Deputy Headteacher:	*Years 1–3.*
Head of English:	*What about staff training?*
Head of Special Needs:	*I would see some kind of school-based INSET for nominated teachers as essential.*
Head of Maths:	*What is the basis for selection?*
Head of Special Needs:	*Up to the department – I'll take anyone.*

4:07

English Teacher gives detailed presentation of two week attachment in industry looking at the nature of written materials used in the company. Study skills are not on the syllabus.

Acting Deputy Headteacher:	*I'd be interested in your report.*

Discussion about how each department can help note-taking and report writing.

Acting Headteacher:	*Could you go to each Head of Department and suggest additions where departments feel they need help?*
English Teacher:	*I'll do that.*
Acting Deputy Headteacher:	*Okay.*

4:16

Deputy Headteacher II gives detailed presentation of returns from departments about INSET requirements.

Deputy Headteacher II:	*We don't know where we go from here because of no LEA guidelines.*
Acting Headteacher:	*I'm going to meeting tomorrow.*
Acting Deputy Headteacher:	*So we've done our list as departments.*

4:21

Acting Deputy:	*Returning to school day. We discussed this at the staff meeting and I asked you to talk in departments.*

Discussion between Acting Headteacher, Head of Special Needs, Deputy Headteacher, Head of 5th Year, Head of Art, Head of Science, Head of Modern Languages about weighting day to morning. Concludes:

Acting Headteacher:	*I'm sure we can change. What I'm saying is in principle do we agree?*
Head of Special Needs:	*I suggest we hold in abeyance because of the new contract.*
Head of Science:	*Go for it.*
Head of 4th/5th Year:	*I agree.*
Head of Maths:	*Maths Department felt it was too long.*
Acting Headteacher:	*Lots of schools work full afternoon.*
Acting Deputy Headteacher:	*We already go 8:55–10:50.*
Acting Headteacher:	*We must rush on.*

4:33

Head of 4th/5th Year:	*Mock exams for 4th Year, can I explain. . . .*
Acting Headteacher:	*Can I thank you for so effectively teaching them.*
Head of 4th/5th Year:	*Discipline in class should go to Head of Department first, not me. Only when need support.*
Various:	*Jokes.*
Acting Deputy Headteacher:	*Any other comments?*
Computer Teacher:	*Exam list has got to be back by end of month.*
Head of Humanities:	*RE should be 2 entries not 1.*
Computer Teacher:	*We'll check.*
Head of Modern Languages:	*I'm organising prize days, anyone know who I can write to for prize money?*
Acting Deputy Headteacher:	*Date next meeting – agreed 5th.*
Head of Science:	*Member of staff back, but not well.*

4:42 close

18 Finance: keeping the books

These materials can be used for opening up the questions of who should be involved in allocating financial resources and how it should be done. Discussion centres round particular examples and a suggested checklist. Ideal group size is between two and ten.

On completion participants should be able to:

a) understand the advantages and disadvantages of involving different groups of people in financial decisions;
b) appreciate that the important decisions in financial matters are management rather than numerical.

Participants will need:
Finance Document I – *Hillside School*
Finance Document II – *Westcliffe School*
Finance Document III – *The checklist*

To the trainer

Once capitation allowances are allocated to a school, it has to be decided how they and other funds are to be divided up between the various sections of the school. We discovered a wide spectrum of ways in which this was done, from the extreme of the Headteacher making all decisions about allocation, with no sharing among other members of staff, to an open Finance Committee debating the issues in great detail.

Schools operate a mixture of strategies, largely by default rather than deliberately. The four different strategies described below are examples suggested by Brian Knight (1983):

1 *Benevolent despotism* occurs where departments may be consulted by a Head or Deputy Head about their plans and requirements, but the money may be allocated out on a grace-and-favour basis in the final analysis, rather than on the basis of real need. The system has potential and can be effective, but is open to abuse via persuasion and wheeler-dealing.

2 *The open market* takes a 'zero-based' budgeting approach, requiring the Head of Department to submit an estimate for every item of new and ongoing departmental expenditure as though it were a brand new department under consideration. Unless care is taken to ensure that estimates are justified and amounts not unduly inflated, this method favours the 'aggressive and wily' at the expense of the 'modest and realistic'.

3 *Creeping incrementalism* is a quick, easy method which adds the inflation amount equally to the previous year's allocation. The method perpetuates previous inequities and makes no allowance for particular needs or new developments.

4 *The formula approach* allocates money out to each subject on the basis of pupil periods and usually a weighting factor reflecting some judgement about the expensiveness of each subject relative to others. Once the initial weightings are agreed, it is a quick – although conservative – method of allocation. One-off requirements would need to be considered separately.

All methods have their advantages and disadvantages – a mixture of strategies makes good sense.

Introduction

1 Generate a discussion about different methods of allocating financial resources.
2 Draw up a table on a flip chart, along the following lines.

System	Method of operating	Controlling agent
Bid – Version 1	Headteacher invites departments to make bids	Headteacher
Bid – Version 2	Committee receives bid	Finance committee
Pupil contact etc	Complex formula etc	Originator of formula etc

3 Discuss the advantages and disadvantages of each of the systems. (About 30 minutes)

Documents I and II

1 Give out copies of Documents I and II. Ask groups to compare the questions asked at **Hillside** with those asked at **Westcliffe**. What systems are they likely to be using? How could they improve the collection of data?

2 Invite groups to design a form together for use in their own school. (At least an hour)

The checklist

Give out copies of the checklist (Document III) and ask groups to use it to evaluate their own system.

Finance Document I: Hillside School

This is the document with which the Headteacher at **Hillside** starts the business of allocating capitation to departments. There is a lot of face-to-face contact with the Headteacher about these allocations. Staff are content with this, since the Headteacher is well respected and inspires confidence.

Departmental allowance this year

I shall be seeing all staff in charge of expenditure after Easter, as usual. Although our capitation is not yet known and will probably not be finalised until May or June, I advise you to start spending as from March.

Work on the assumption of a similar allowance to that in previous years, but confine your initial spending to half that amount, pending our discussion.

Please bring *written* coverage of the points below for discussion after Easter.

1 Allowance last year

2 Approximate spending (as applicable) in last year (rough figures only)

    a) Hardware – equipment
    b) Software – CAL, A/V
    c) Stationery (additional to centralised order)
    d) Textual resources
    e) Materials – repro, etc
    f) Rentals – contracts
    g) Maintenance
    h) Other areas (specify)

3 Priority areas of funding last year, especially those which were given specific allowances.

4 Developmental areas funded last year.

5 Priority areas for funding this year.

6 Developmental areas desirable in this year.

7 A list of planned purchases for this year – in order of priority.

Please ensure I have *written* coverage of the above for records either at our meeting or (preferably) before it.

Finance Document II: Westcliffe School

The Deputy Head responsible for finance at **Westcliffe** circulated a suggested proforma for requests for the coming year, which he then compared with the previous year's estimated allocation. This proforma is as follows.

SUGGESTED PROFORMA FOR FACULTY ESTIMATE FOR EXPENDITURE

STATIONERY

TEXTBOOKS   6TH FORM TEXTBOOKS

AV HARD AND SOFTWARE

REPROGRAPHICS

NEW EQUIPMENT

CONSUMABLES (sic)

REPLACEMENTS

NEW COURSES

ANY OTHER ITEMS

                                           FINAL TOTAL

Any additional information may be attached in the usual way.

Finance Document III: The checklist

1 Who has a say? Is it just the Head? If it is devolved to a committee, are only senior staff allowed to serve on it? What about governors? What about non-teaching staff?

2 Who else gets to know about it? Once decisions are made, how well are they made public?

3 Are governors or the PTA involved? How often are governors briefed on the system and its implementation? How are governors' own funds incorporated into the capitation system? How does the PTA decide how to spend its money?

4 How are new staff initiated into the whole system? Is there a finance section in the staff handbook? Are answers to *all* questions in this section dealt with fully?

5 What percentage of the total capitation is set aside? On what terms? Is this availability widely known? When is the contingency brought back to the general fund?

6 Do new Heads of Department have an extra allocation? Is this allocation for both internal and external appointees? Is the system explained to candidates for appointments?

7 Is there a development allowance? Who decides on how it is spent? How does the school use its finances to foster change or growth?

8 How are unofficial and extra funds integrated into the system? Do departments raise their own income? What fraction of what they raise do they keep? How is this money audited? What grants do advisers make? How are such grants allowed for? Are they made public?

9 How do staff arrange for money to be spent? Is the Head the only signatory? Do staff write out their own orders? Who keeps the order books?

10 How is the spending monitored? How often do departments get a statement of their expenditure? How much warning do people get when they are close to their spending limit? What arrangements are made for countermanding orders? Is a contingency fund maintained?

11 Is the system vulnerable to absence of key personnel? Who is the back-up for the Bursar or secretary who runs the system? Is there a Vice-Chairman for the committee?

19 Core and periphery staff: their different needs

The aim of this chapter is to raise awareness of an aspect of school management which is not often considered. The terms 'core' and 'periphery' will probably not be familiar to staff in this context. We suggest a small group (5–10) of senior staff including those with particular responsibility for probationers, temporary and part-time staff and students. If it is difficult to identify such staff, that is the first lesson learned!

On completion participants will be able to:

a) distinguish core from periphery staff;
b) describe strategies for dealing with the two different categories.

Participants will need:
Core/periphery Document I: *Hall End*

To the trainer

In the 1980s commercial organisations have increasingly tended to have two categories of employee: a small core of staff who have the key skills and knowledge crucial to the business and a wide range of peripheral people, who may or may not be direct employees (Atkinson, 1984). Members of the first group are highly regarded by the employer, well paid and involved in those activities that are unique to the firm or give it a distinctive character. They have good career prospects and offer the employer an important contribution that cannot come from elsewhere.

Those in the peripheral category are in two broad groups: first, those who have skills that are needed but which are not specific to the particular firm, like word processing, catering or driving heavy goods vehicles; second, those without highly-developed skills, who are likely to be engaged on short-term contracts. This core/peripheral tendency has led to the development of many agencies, consultancies and small businesses which specialise in the supply of peripheral personnel.

This practice is anathema to many people in education, especially as it seems to strike at the root of the idea of school culture. There is, however, a long tradition of employing peripatetic staff in schools to deal with specialised subjects and casual staff to provide cover. There are signs that the core/periphery divide may become more common as schools seek the same types of flexibility that other undertakings have been trying to achieve.

The three most common types of periphery staff, both teaching and non-teaching, are:

- those who have temporary appointments;
- those who work part-time;
- those on supply.

Other peripheral groups are peripatetic staff, voluntary groups who work with the school, contract dinner people, students and advisory teachers. Other aspects of school organisation that raise the same issues are consortium arrangements and TVEI relationships with colleges.

Management issues associated with periphery staff

Provide all group members with a copy of Document I – Hall End and develop a discussion about the core/periphery issues raised by it.
Some issues we found were,

1 There was a need for clear instructions about the syllabus content, methodology and discipline procedures used in the schools if the pupils were to receive anything consistently. This was met by a very large staff handbook and a great deal of written materials, work books and schemes for the pupils.

2 There was a need to recognise that the core staff, particularly main grade teachers, were primarily involved in assisting periphery teachers as it was they who were sharing the classes and doing most of the teaching. These core staff felt aggrieved because this additional work was not recognised.

3 Senior staff spent a lot of time on periphery staff; for example, one of the Deputies dealt with all students, a Deputy, Senior Teacher and Head of Department spent much time dealing with supply teachers and the Headteacher and a Deputy dealt with college staff, especially on TVEI matters. This high degree of preoccupation with those on the periphery led to core staff often feeling neglected and taken-for-granted.

4 Out of 55 core staff, 42 are either probationers or main grade teachers without extra responsibilities. The other 13 feel ignored by the management, organisation and administration of the school. Yet

they have the heaviest teaching loads and act as tutors, so they have to deal extensively with peripheral staff on tutorial and specialist subject matters. This group of staff included those who were felt to have problems such as personal, health and class control. Were these the casualties of a school with high professional standards and high numbers of peripheral staff?

(30 minutes)

Managing the core and periphery

Taking the issues generated above, try to elicit examples of how this might be managed. Examples we found were:

At **Westcliffe School** there was one part-time secretary, based in the Lower School. Dora, the Registrar, started the day three mornings a week in the Lower School to ensure the secretary knew what was going on and had everything she needed. It was partly a social visit and partly business.

At **William Barnes School** each supply teacher was given a box in the morning which contained a map of the school, a timetable, a list of staff to contact (with their extension numbers), an abbreviated staff handbook, paper, pencils and materials for the day's lessons. As one supply teacher said to us, 'I love coming here'.

At **Westcliffe School** subject meetings were held when the part-time staff were in school. This gave them the opportunity to contribute and understand developments.

This and other experience gives rise to the following ideas:

1 To make the most of skilled peripheral staff (like peripatetic and supply teachers) it is necessary to specify what is needed from them as closely as possible. The emphasis is on output rather than input: what is required *from* them rather than on *how* they should do it. You take the 'how' for granted because they are skilled people and will reduce their confidence and their contribution if you specify the how rather than the what.

2 Whole jobs are better than bits and pieces. Thought can usually eliminate the baby-sitting risk of deploying supply staff only to keep children quiet and replace the bits and pieces with a request to teach a specific part of the syllabus, assess the children's understanding at the end and leave a copy of the results. This makes it useful for the children, worthwhile for the supply teacher, who has been able to do more than just hold the fort, and useful for the subject teacher, who does not spend 15 minutes on return from sick leave finding out what

was done yesterday and making disparaging inferences about it.

3 Peripheral staff are nearly always emotionally detached from the school and do not have the same single-minded commitment that is likely from core staff. They will therefore expect to fit their contribution to your requirements, whatever their personal views about school culture, discipline and so forth. Attempts to involve them more fully may be unsuccessful as their commitment is to the job they do rather than to the school; their personal motivational needs are different from those of core staff and the nature of their potential contribution is also different.

4 Peripheral staff need clear guidance on the everyday trivialities that everyone else takes for granted: the location of the lavatories, where to get coffee, who does the washing up, local conventions on dress, which chairs are 'special' in the common room, rules on discipline and so forth.

5 Core staff are actually or potentially committed to the school and need a different type of valuing from peripheral employees. Although the core staff will have the same needs for confirmation that they are doing a good technical job, they will also need valuing as people and will focus on the school as the arena for *all* their professional hopes and ambitions. That valuing is needed also to ensure the proper briefing of peripheral staff and the effective consolidation of their contribution. Members of the core are at all levels in the hierarchy and all of them are needed to enable the periphery to do a proper job.

6 No matter how rare and mysterious the skills to be brought in on the periphery, those in the core must have sufficient expertise to specify and manage the peripheral contribution, otherwise there is a serious risk that the tail will wag the dog. In a tight-knit culture like a school there is no place for the maverick expert.

7 Those who come in to the school, without being committed to it, also go out, taking an opinion about the school and about education. Some of those on the periphery are not professionals; they may make a whole set of stereotyped judgements about education on the basis of a single experience. A significant proportion of students in teacher training either abandon their courses or do not enter the profession on graduation, and the main reason is that they are discouraged not by the children, but by the teachers.

(About 45 minutes)

Reference

Atkinson, J 'Manpower Strategies for Flexible Organisations', in *Personnel Management*, August, 1984.

Core/periphery Document I: Hall End

An example of a school with a lot of staff on the periphery whose main loyalty is outside the school.

At this school there were eight people on acting points for various reasons. Some permanent staff were on secondment to the LEA as advisory teachers, two were on maternity leave and the school staff was due to contract because of falling rolls. For similar reasons there were eight basic grade teachers on temporary appointments to the school whilst the changes took place. The school had a large number of supply teachers in most days, as many as 15 was quite normal, to cover for TVEI, illness, attendance at courses and unfilled vacancies. The school had several classes taught by staff from a college who were on the same site as the school. In addition, there was a rapid turnover of staff, first because promotion was relatively easy for staff from this school as they had experience of many of the progressive aspects of education and, secondly, because it was a difficult setting and many staff wanted to teach in rather more salubrious areas. When asked, the Headteacher did not know how many teaching staff there were. Sitting in the staffroom it was often unclear who was a member of staff. What was clear was who the core of full-time permanent staff were.

This situation created particular management and organisational issues.
● What do you think these might be?

20 Communications III: the briefing meeting

This is a straightforward method of deciding how to introduce briefing meetings into a school and can be undertaken by any size group of staff, with a series of practical questions to work through.

On completion participants should be able to:

a) decide what type of meeting to introduce;
b) decide how often it should take place;
c) decide how it should be run.

Participants will need:
Briefing Document I – *Briefing meeting issues*

To the trainer

The main substance of the training session is to consider the questions in Document I. The trainer should introduce the discussion by setting out the particular question that is appropriate for the school. This will normally be, 'Do we want to introduce briefing meetings?', but in some circumstances briefing meetings may already be running but be in need of review. It may also help the discussion to provide some bare facts about what the MOSS researchers found. This information lends itself to OHP or flip chart presentation.

In the schools studied the MOSS researchers found widespread use of short staff meetings, daily or weekly, as an important feature of school communications, in conjunction with a staff bulletin. The incidence was:

Daily meeting and weekly bulletin	3 schools
Weekly meeting and weekly bulletin	8 schools
Weekly meeting and daily bulletin	1 school
Weekly meeting and no bulletin	1 school
Daily bulletin and no meeting	2 schools
Weekly bulletin and no meeting	6 schools
No bulletin and no meeting	3 schools

The reasons for holding the meetings varied, and often meetings achieved objectives different from those intended. It was concluded that the meetings fulfilled one or more of seven different purposes:

1 *Information* The nominal function of the meeting was invariably to inform members of staff of news (mainly about children), and points of general interest, such as expected visitors. There were also reminders of matters in the bulletin.

2 *Organisational cohesion* The regular meeting reinforced the personal identification of each staff member with the community of individuals making up the staff body, and with their shared purpose in pursuing school aims and objectives. In this way it was similar to school assembly, and the symbolic presence of the Headteacher and senior staff was an important element.

3 *Social cohesion* Although similar, a different purpose is the refreshing of acquaintanceships and the exchange of gossip between people who would otherwise seldom meet. This assists the social integration of newcomers and can sustain the understanding between established members of staff. It is especially useful when two staffs are being merged. Although this is a part of the general function of the staffroom, social cohesion needs careful reinforcement with large staffs operating across two or more sites, and timetabling arrangements which isolate some individuals and groups. The hectic nature of many teachers' school days means that they never use the staffroom other than to attend meetings. Social cohesion is helped by the extrovert staffroom characters who lighten the atmosphere and develop cameraderie through jokes and banter.

4 *'The trading floor'* The regular, formal gathering provides an opportunity for many rapid, mini-meetings between individuals, both before and after the official business is complete. Meeting dates are arranged, deals are struck ('Will you do my ... if I do your...?'), information is exchanged, new members of staff are introduced to those outside their departmental circle, in an atmosphere reminiscent of a stock exchange.

5 *Ritual celebrations* Among the announcements are items which all present 'celebrate', such as welcomes and farewells, which are more than arrivals and departures. The collective celebration of good news helps to reinforce social cohesion.

6 *Developing and disseminating the school ethos* There is the opportunity to disseminate and develop the school ethos by demonstrating priorities and endorsing certain norms which are valued within the school, such as timekeeping, style of speaking to people, openness, asking for help, attitudes on school uniform and so forth.

7 *Testing reaction* Any member of staff contemplating an initiative

may float the idea at the morning meeting to estimate the degree of enthusiasm it evokes.

How to set up the meeting

1 Distribute Document I and allow 10 minutes reading time before developing the discussion.
2 Work through the various discussion points systematically and then summarise the action that is being agreed, together with notes about who will do what.

Briefing Document I: Briefing meeting issues

How to set up a daily or weekly staff meeting

The following questions are intended to help you review the arrangements for meetings already held, or to consider their introduction.

1 *What is the relationship of the meeting to the bulletin?*

Most schools have daily or weekly bulletins, containing much of the routine information which is potential material for the meetings. Despite the danger of merely reiterating what has already been written and circulated, there is a constructive interrelationship between written and spoken communication, as suggested by ACAS:

> Face-to-face communication is direct and swift. It should enable discussion, questioning and feedback to take place but ought to be supplemented by written material where information is detailed or complex and where records are important. (ACAS, 1984, p. 13)

One possibility is for the bulletin to follow the meeting, containing a summary of the main points or further particulars of some of the matters mentioned.

Another aspect of the connection between the meeting and the bulletin is the human long-term and short-term memory. Quite extensive and detailed information may be retained after reading the bulletin, but then 'forgotten' until recalled by announcements in the meeting. A brief announcement can recall a great deal of information, and information that was not retained will be looked up after the trigger of an announcement.

A daily/weekly meeting does not make the bulletin obsolete, but can necessitate changes in the bulletin's format and content.

2 *How often should meetings be held?*

The choice seems to lie between weekly or daily, with most schools opting for weekly. Daily meetings are better for speeding the communication flow and providing effective recall of information already circulated. They provide a prompt, co-ordinated start to the working day that is to follow, and have to be short and very well organised.

Weekly meetings do not offer the same recall facility but avoid the risk of a meeting without sufficient business to justify it. A ten minute meeting of a staff of 60 consumes ten teaching staff hours: more than a day's teaching.

The final decision between weekly or daily will rest on what the staff will accept and the ease or difficulty of gathering staff at the meeting place.

3 *How long should meetings be?*

Daily meetings little more than five minutes; weekly meetings no more than 15. Briefing meetings rarely last longer and the short, snappy meeting enables people to be reminded or informed of a few things which they will remember without having to make notes.

4 *When should meetings takes place?*

Meetings are usually at the beginning of the school day, although there are examples of meetings at other times, especially weekly meetings. There are advantages in 'getting set' for the coming day. Weekly meetings are usually on Monday, occasionally on Friday.

5 *Where should the meeting be held?*

Although the meeting would normally be in the staffroom, not all staffrooms are appropriate. The setting needs to be one where most people can see everyone else and where there will not be interruptions from telephones, clattering coffee cups or other distractions, so that all present can concentrate for a short time on a rapid exchange of information, including non-verbal communication. It may not be essential for all those attending to be sitting down.

6 *How should the meeting be run?*

Methods of conducting the meeting vary considerably, but usually begin with Head's announcements, which are either reminders or items of news. These announcements do not have to be made by the Head and a useful way of emphasising the collective responsibility of the Senior Management Group is for each member to take it in turn to run the meeting. The next item could be questions about the announcements, but questions only for information, not for discussion at this type of meeting. Then there could be announcements from other members of staff relating to events in the day which is about to begin. A refinement is to have an agenda which varies slightly day by day. There has to be a restriction on the nature of exchanges, and some subjects, like school uniform, have to be taboo for these meetings. The important principle is to manage the meetings so that each one is seen as being useful by at least most of those who attend, starting promptly and moving briskly.

7 *Who should attend the meeting?*

Attendance may be either compulsory or voluntary-but-expected for members of the teaching staff. When voluntary, the meeting will in practice be attended by the great majority of staff because of the benefits which they personally derive from attending. Unless they are out of school, it is imperative that all members of the Senior Management Group attend, for the symbolic reasons mentioned earlier. Those not personally running the meeting that day will be in demand on 'the trading floor' immediately afterwards. A more difficult question is about attendance by non-teaching staff. In some schools they do not attend at all, in others they are represented by one or two key figures, such as the bursar, caretaker and librarian. Another possibility is for the Head's secretary to attend, take notes and prepare a follow-up bulletin. One view is that non-teaching staff should not be excluded, but another possibility is that non-teaching staff would find the proceedings largely irrelevant to their needs, once the novelty had worn off. Also some – like laboratory assistants – will find that the busiest part of their day coincides with the meeting.

8 *How do you cope with a split site?*

There is an obvious problem where the school is on a split site, yet this is the sort of situation in which such meetings are most valuable. With weekly meetings there can be a duplication with, say, a meeting on Monday at one site and Friday at the other. The bulletin then provides a common feature between the two. An alternative is for meetings on the two sites to be held at the same time, with one of the Deputies acting as regular, local leader and the Head and other members of the Senior Management Team attending each meeting alternately.

21 The poor performer: the hardest problem to tackle

This closing chapter provides an introduction to one of the hardest of all management problems in schools. The structure for the discussion can suggest ways of tackling the problems and a range of explanations. The exercise is suitable for anyone having responsibility for others and is best developed in group discussion between five or six people.

On completion participants will be able to:

a) distinguish the stages of establishing a gap between expected and actual performance;
b) establish reasons for poor performance;
c) work out ways of dealing with poor performance.

Participants will need:
Poor performer Document I – *Poor performers*
Poor performer Document II – *Reasons for poor performance*
Poor performer Document III – *Checklist*

To the trainer

We have all worked with someone whose work was inadequate. We are often sympathetic if it is a temporary, personal problem and we know our colleague will make a good contribution as soon as it is possible. We all work badly sometimes because the organisation of our work is poor either because of others' carelessness or our own errors. We find there is no classroom available, there are no pencils left, the video has not been returned, the temporary huts were poorly constructed so we cannot hear the children at the back speak, or we have forgotten the books . . . But the poor performer whom we all complain of most is the individual with a long-term history of not working as well as is normal n the particular setting. This section is about dealing with problems of ndividual poor performance; not the performance of a group within a chool or of the whole school.

ntroduction – the problem

)evelop a general discussion and elicit some examples of poor perform- nce. The research findings below may provide a useful basis.

We found problems, both long- and short-term, with individual erformance at all levels in the schools we visited. Like all human ctivity, teaching has a few who, for various reasons, are not coping /ith their present jobs. Many of these people were receiving sympathe- c support from their colleagues, although some had long presented roblems that had not yet been tackled.

Most of us do not perform equally well in all parts of our work. Vhere there are *specific difficulties* within an overall excellent perform- nce, these are often easiest to remedy. For example, one of the leadteachers we observed was poor at personal communication. This ras understood within the school and compensated for by other nembers of the senior staff taking on this role. Another Headteacher ras very poor at managing the process of change despite a very exciting genda for change within the school. Several well-established Heads of epartment were beginning to explain to him how he might handle the tuation better.

We also came across examples where people had been *unable to keep p with the changes*. For example, the Head of Music who thought nusic was singing lessons and listening to music composed before the ventieth century and who rarely arrived in school on time, or the Head f Business Studies who had got left behind by the computing technolo- y and expertise now demanded of his department (although he ran a ery good typing department). One Registrar was keeping detailed :cords of the school's finances that required her entering the same gures in three different books. On the desk in front of her sat a new 3M computer supplied by the LEA – untouched. People of this ategory can be the most frustrating to their colleagues but bring out /mpathy from those less involved. Downward mobility could assist 1any people who find themselves in this situation.

Some other poor performers were those who had been *over- romoted* or whose performance had tailed off since being in this post. or example, one Deputy Head was seen by his colleagues as doing very ttle and was himself waiting for early retirement: he was 53. One :nior teacher we met had been an Acting Head of Lower School for a :ar during a period of reorganisation. She was not finally appointed to the post but given a senior teacher post without specific responsibilities. She looked around for odd jobs but they were never very substantial. In most schools we found one of the senior posts had very little substance; this suggests that seven senior staff is too many for most schools.

Others were obviously struggling for a variety of *personal* reasons. One Head of Art had abdicated the promotion of his Department's work to the others whilst he coped with his drink problem. One English and Drama teacher was constantly late and disorganised with serious class control problems. As always, it is the weakest who have the most trouble: 'Teachers who cannot control classes find they have to combat more misbehaviour than others' (Reid *et al.*, 1987).

Establishing the gap

There are both quantity and quality problems with people's performance. Some just do not do enough, others do things badly – some even manage to do too little, badly!

Before anything can be done about poor performance it is important to establish a gap between required performance and actual performance. The work that is expected is communicated to individuals through job descriptions, school handbooks which outline roles and procedures, and also orally at meetings and between individuals. There may be reasons for poor performance where any of these are inadequately used. To establish what the actual performance is we need to look at records such as sickness and absence, personal files, unfinished work, complaints from parents and observations from colleagues and Heads of Department.

It is also important to compare the performance with others doing similar work – is it very much worse? – and talk to a variety of colleagues who come into contact with the individual.

Take one or two of the examples generated by the previous discussion and decide at least three possible ways of establishing a gap in their performance between expected and actual behaviour. If you prefer to use our examples, use Document I or the examples from chapter 9, 'Job definition and individual feedback'.

(About 30 minutes.)

Reasons for the gap

Having established a gap between actual and required performance the next step is to look at the reasons for this gap.

1 Get the group to brainstorm (see Introduction, 'How to use this book') possible reasons for poor performance. (About 15 minutes.)
2 Organise the ideas into three categories: personal, organisation and individual.
3 Distribute Document II.
4 Compare your brainstorm examples with those in Document II.
5 Discuss the differences and similarities (15 minutes).

Dealing with poor performance

The two stages of establishing a gap and the reason, or reasons, for poor performance are only important in so far as they serve the main objective of dealing with the poor performance, that is, improving it. Ways of dealing with it will suggest themselves once the reasons are clear.

Get the group to give suggestions about what they would do for each of the reasons generated above or concentrate on one or two. (This can take 30 minutes or longer.)

Emphasise at the end that all are best done by setting joint goals together with the poor performer in some face-to-face interview. The aim should be to set jointly agreed, reasonable goals and a date to review the performance. Who does this depends on the roles of subordinates, colleagues, Heads of Department, Deputy Headteachers, Headteachers, as we discuss in Part II.

At the end, give each member Document III as a personal checklist.

References

Hargreaves, D (1967), *Social Relations in a Secondary School*, London: RKP.

Hargreaves, D (1972), *Interpersonal Relations and Education*, London: RKP.

Reid, K, Hopkins, D and Holly, P (1987), *Towards the Effective School*, Oxford: Basil Blackwell.

Stewart, V and A (1982), *Managing the Poor Performer*, Gower.

Video Arts (1984), *So You Think You Can Manage?* Methuen.

Poor performer Document I: Poor performers

- *A Head of Music* who thought music was singing lessons and listening to music composed before the twentieth century and who rarely arrived in school on time.

- The *Head of Business Studies* who had got left behind by the computing technology and expertise now demanded of his department (although he ran a very good typing department).

- One *Registrar* was keeping detailed records of the school's finances that required her entering the same figures in three different books. On the desk in front of her sat a new IBM computer supplied by the LEA – untouched.

- A *Head of Art* had abdicated the promotion of his Department's work to the others whilst he coped with his drink problem.

- One *English and Drama teacher* was constantly late and disorganised with serious class control problems.

- The *Bursar's* understanding of her role (and, perhaps, her personality) made it difficult for her to delegate responsibility to other non-teaching staff. She simply did not trust other people to do things properly. In the caretaker's own very perceptive words, 'She creates her own problems by keeping too many fingers in too many pies. Staff have to go to her first if they want a light bulb changed and I'm not allowed to order my own stuff.' Nobody in the school seemed prepared to take on the 'redoubtable Mrs M', whilst admitting that she was a liability. The Head's problem was partly his own pusillanimity but also the weaknesses of his own Deputy – the Head of Administration. Neither were prepared to confront the Bursar. From the Head's point of view the answer lay in waiting for both Bursar and Head of Administration to retire, 'When they go, things will be different'. He also observed that the other Deputies were too busy in their pastoral/academic roles to relieve the Bursar and the Head of Administration of some of the more sensitive 'management' tasks.

Poor performer Document II: Reasons for poor performance

1 *Personal* reasons outside the school's control:
Intellectual ability
Physical ability
Emotional stability
Domestic circumstances
Family break-up
Health

2 *Organisational* reasons outside the individual's control:
Job assigned
Job changed
Pay
Poor discipline
Lack of investment in equipment
Poor physical conditions
Lack of or inappropriate training
Planning or improvisation
Poor management
Location and transport difficulties

3 *Individual* reasons arising from a mismatch with the school:
Poor understanding of the job
Sense of fair play abused
Lack of motivation
Personality clashes within the group or with superiors
Inappropriate levels of confidence
Conflict of religious or moral values
Group dynamics
Training programme misunderstood

Poor performer Document III: Checklist

1 How do those working with you know what you expect them to do?

2 What opportunity is there for you to discuss whether the work you expect is possible? (Include formal and informal opportunities.)

3 What records do you keep about the work of those you are responsible for? Who has access to them?

4 Do you have someone you regard as a poor performer working for you at the moment? If so:
   - Have you talked to them about it?
   - Have you established a gap between expected and actual performance?
   - Are the reasons personal, organisational or individual, or a mixture?
   - Try setting joint goals and a review date together.

5 Are there any aspects of your work which you know you are doing less well than you ought? Why do you think this might be? What might help you to resolve these problems?